Blue Genes

Blue Genes

Breaking free from the chemical imbalances
that affect your moods, your mind,
your life, and your loved ones

Paul Meier, M.D.,
Todd Clements, M.D.,
Jean-Luc Bertrand, D.M.D. David Mandt, Sr., M.A.

TYNDALE™
MOMENTUM

An Imprint of
Tyndale House Publishers, Inc.

Visit Tyndale online at www.tyndale.com.

Visit Tyndale Momentum online at www.tyndalemomentum.com.

TYNDALE is a registered trademark of Tyndale House Publishers, Inc. *Tyndale Momentum* and the Tyndale Momentum logo are trademarks of Tyndale House Publishers, Inc. Tyndale Momentum is an imprint of Tyndale House Publishers, Inc.

Blue Genes

The case examples presented in this book are fictional composites based on the authors' clinical experience with hundreds of clients through the years. All names are invented, and any resemblance between these fictional characters and actual persons is coincidental.

Library of Congress Cataloging-in-Publication Data
Blue genes / Paul Meier ... [et al.].
    p. cm.
  ISBN 978-1-4143-1216-3 (sc)
  1. Affective disorders—Genetic aspects. 2. Affective disorders—Religious aspects—Christianity.
I. Meier, Paul D.
  RC455.4.G4B58 2006
  616.89'5042—dc22

                          2006002587

Printed in the United States of America

17 16 15 14
 7   6   5   4   3

Contents

When you get tired of your old blue *jeans,* you can turn them into cut-offs or cleaning rags, or else throw them away and buy a new pair. But what can you do about the *genes* you can't throw out? You may grow tired of the genes in the DNA you inherited from your parents, but you can't change them or toss them away. The same goes for the genes in the DNA you may pass on to your children and the genes in the DNA of friends or loved ones.

The genes you inherit are yours for life, and they influence almost everything about you: your height, metabolism, color and amount of hair, eye color and left- or right-handedness, for instance. Your genes modulate even nonphysical attributes such as intelligence, special gifts and abilities, musical and athletic potential, mental handicaps, or perfectionism. Many researchers now believe most of our personality traits are genetically determined.

What you may not realize is how the genes you inherit also strongly influence your psyche, or moods. Genetics dynamically contribute to your daily brain functioning, specifically by controlling the balance of four vital brain chemicals (otherwise known as neurotransmitters). These four key chemicals—serotonin, norepinephrine, dopamine, and GABA (gamma-aminobutyric acid)—are responsible for influencing your ability to experience love, joy, peace, patience, gentleness, humility, energy, motivation, memorization, concentration, a positive attitude, self-acceptance, your dreams, and sanity itself.

What happens when a person's genes or other factors result in brain chemical abnormalities? The list of problems stemming from "blue genes" includes depression, anxiety, bipolar disorder, panic attacks, substance abuse, ADHD (attention-deficit, hyperactivity disorder), psychosis, low self-esteem, and inability to get along with others. Millions of people in our society are predisposed to these and other difficulties, thanks in part to their "blue genes." Yet they are not condemned to suffer unaided; there is hope for healing.

Your brain is so complex it makes the most sophisticated computer in the world look like a junky, old adding machine. It would take a computer programmer over a hundred years to train a computer to do what the mind of a one-year-old infant is capable of. While scientists continue to discover new brain chemicals and determine what functions they perform, there is still a vast amount we don't yet understand about the brain. We do know there are more than the four key neurotransmitters mentioned above, additional brain chemicals that also affect mood and behavior. This book focuses on the four most-studied brain amines (chemicals that enable us to have thoughts, choices, and feelings), and seeks to understand the powerful roles they play in everyday functioning.

YOUR LIFE STORY

As important as they are, however, genetics and brain chemicals do not tell your entire story. The person that you are is actually determined by a combination of genes, environment (including God), and the choices you make. Human behavior is much more complex than genetics alone. God made us in His image, not as robots, but with free will, so do not think that genetics is the most important of the three factors which largely determine who we are.

A personal friendship with the God who created our genes in the first place is by far the most important factor in our lives. Yet it's important to recognize that our genes—including our "blue genes"—and our environments, especially early childhood environmental influences, contribute greatly not only to who we are, but also to how we see and interpret our relationships with God Himself.

Research shows that a young child saying good-night prayers to his or her Heavenly Father is unconsciously thinking, "Dear Heavenly Version of my earthly father." Such is the influence of family dynamics on spiritual development. On the other hand, a person inheriting a low serotonin level will automatically lean toward thinking he or she is and always will be unacceptable to God—too imperfect to measure up. Or if someone inherits a dopamine abnormality, that person may very well think he or she actually *is* God.

God has created each reader of this book to be unique. There never has been, nor will there ever be, another you! No other person will ever live the same experiences and face the same life choices as you will. The challenges faced by each of us, and those we love, however, are at the same time deeply individualized and reassuringly common.

This book was written to offer practical help. The authors will present the latest information on helping you, your family members, and other loved ones turn "blue genes" into "joy genes." We hope to increase the joy and meaning in your life and improve relationships with those you love—as well as with the One who designed and created the very genes passed down by your ancestors to you.

We wish you and your family a happy journey as you proceed to learn more about what makes your genes fit and how to get the best wear from them—for life.

Chapter One

Blue Genes: Hope and Healing for You and Your Family

When I taught counseling to future pastors at Trinity Seminary in Chicago, most of my students were loving, joyful, family-oriented, practical people, eager to bring joy to others. But I repeatedly noticed one very sad student, Charles Rausch. Not all my students laughed at my jokes, but I never saw Charles crack a smile at a joke or for any reason.

I felt so sorry for Charles, I asked him if we could talk after class about his future, and he reluctantly agreed. I grabbed his student file, rushed to my office, and met him there. From his file I learned that Charles was married to an E.R. nurse and had three children, one for each year of the marriage so far. The family was living in poverty, with the couple refusing financial assistance from either set of parents, who had offered their help.

I checked the test Charles had taken upon application to Trinity Seminary: the MMPI, the main psychological personality test given around the world. The results in Charles' case were somewhat shocking. He came out in the ninety-ninth percentile for depression and masochism (the need to suffer).

I told Charles, "Man, with an MMPI like this, I'll bet you are planning on becoming a missionary to Ethiopia."

"I am," he replied.

I assured Charles, "There is absolutely nothing wrong with going to help the good people of Ethiopia if God calls you to do that. But I just want you to think about whether you are being called to Ethiopia by God—or by your demanding mother!"

After seeing Charles weekly for counseling, I discovered Charles had an extensive family history of depression, with many relatives on both sides of his family tree who suffered from it. So I persuaded Charles to take an antidepressant for his inherited "blue genes," in his case, chronic dysthymia.

—PAUL MEIER, M.D.

His "blue genes" were responsible for blocking Charles' path to happiness; clearly, he's not alone. The nation's attention was drawn to the same subject on January 17, 2005, when *Time* magazine devoted half of its subject matter to the topic of "blue genes." In-depth articles discussed happiness, depression and what the latest research reveals about genetic tendencies toward depression, the role of serotonin, and people's attitudes about inherited brain abnormalities.

The magazine cover featured a brightly colored smiley face and the word "happiness" in big print. Compelling questions leaped from the cover: "Is joy in your genes?" "Does God want us to be happy?"

What do you think about those questions?

In a message on Psalm 19 at the Stonebriar Community Church in Frisco, Texas, Dr. Stan Toussaint (substituting for my regular pastor, Dr. Chuck Swindoll) detailed God's purposes for giving mankind the Holy

Scriptures. The number one reason is to restore our souls. God's second purpose for giving us the Bible is to teach us wisdom, how to survive in this complex world. And God's third purpose, according to Psalm 19, is "happiness."

The New Testament tells us that God became man, Jesus Christ, to enable us to have abundant lives. Additionally, when a person develops the fruit of the Spirit of God, he or she should have love rather than hatred, prejudice and bitterness. We will have happiness rather than depression. We will have peace rather than anxiety.

Does God want us to be happy? Of course He does. Our happiness is not His primary concern, but it is part of His plan for us. Some religious legalists teach the opposite of Scripture: desiring happiness is somehow a sin, and a truly spiritual person will live like the monk in a cave, with a ten-year vow of silence, suffering daily while walking miles in the hot sun just to get some bread and water.

Wouldn't it be better for that monk to give up his masochism and pride in his "super spirituality" and get out in the real world to help restore the souls of unhappy people? In psychiatry this phenomenon is called a "reaction formation." In other words, some people are so arrogant that they have a reaction formation and go to great extremes to prove to themselves and others that they are extremely humble when they are not. If a husband keeps accusing his wife of having an affair, for example, he is almost certainly struggling against those acts himself. If a preacher preaches against the same sin every week, he is probably enmeshed in that sin himself, or a similar sin.

THE ROAD TO HAPPINESS: MARY'S STORY

It's not wrong to be happy. Charles himself eventually found that balance in his life, thanks to a combination of medication and counseling. In his case, both treatments were required, though millions can be helped with medication alone, on the one hand, or counseling alone, on the other.

In fact, for some people the physical and mental "relief" from anti-depressants, sleeping pills or tranquilizers actually discourages them from looking inward. Their motivation to discover repressed emotions, improve environmental factors, and make wise life choices actually diminishes. Many of these people could work to heal relationships, change thought patterns, or confront problems by going to counseling. These changes actually have the ability to correct brain chemistry without medication.

Mary Mullens was a good example of that. Mary was a 46-year-old homemaker who had lifelong depression and who, since her teen years, had been treated by family doctors with a wide variety of psychiatric medi-cations, which provided only minimal relief from her suicidal urges. She came to the Meier Day Program in the Dallas area, hoping to receive just the right combination of medications to finally rid her of her depression.

But the more her counselors got to know Mary, through seven hours a day of group, educational and individual counseling, the clearer it was that her problem was not genetic. Her father was a chauvinistic, critical, domineering man. Her mother was passive. Mary, like 85 percent of human beings, had married someone very much like her parent of the opposite sex—a critical, controlling attorney.

In all her thirty years of unsuccessfully trying antidepressant medica-tion, Mary had never received insight-oriented counseling. But she was swamped with it for three straight weeks in the Day Program.

Throughout her treatment, Mary wept often, forgave her parents and others, reprogrammed her brain, and learned to stand up to the control of her father and husband. By the end of three weeks, she had recovered from her depression for the first time in her life.

Her husband regretted the day he brought Mary to the clinic. He lost control of his former slave, and even threatened to sue the clinic, but changed his mind when he found out what Mary had said about his many marital abuses. She refused to live with him unless he got extensive help, and it finally dawned on him what a jerk he had been all his life. After a few months of marital counseling, they moved back in together and have built quite a reasonable marriage in the past few years.

In a recent follow-up counseling session, Mary said her husband had been treating her well for several years now, in contrast to the years of verbal and even occasional physical abuse preceding his repentance. She said with a smile on her face, "He finally realized how much he really loves me and wants me to be there with him the rest of his life."

Counseling such as Mary's can lead to breakthroughs, but other factors also contribute. Dietary influences, for instance, may improve mental functioning by altering brain chemicals. Physicians have known for decades that the proper diet can make a difference in some depressed adults and children. Chapter 10 of this book contains a detailed picture of the way the food, nutrients, and vitamins we consume affect the brain.

WHAT MODERN MEDICINES CAN DO

In addition to counseling and nutrition, today an array of medications provides hope for those suffering from mental health disorders.

As medical knowledge rapidly progresses, researchers theorize that many mental health disorders may be due, in part, to genetic factors. The January 17 *Time* magazine articles estimated that up to 50 percent of the world's population might have an underlying genetic propensity for mental health problems.

That means the 50 percent of those of us "lucky enough" to have blue genes often suffer from more psychiatric problems than the other half of the population. We are more prone to depression, sadness and anger, especially under stressful circumstances. The way our brains handle stress leads to abnormalities in the four major brain chemicals needed to prevent depression and anxiety. About 20 percent of the population either requires lifelong psychiatric medications to avoid depression and other mental disorders, or they would enjoy great benefits from modern-day psychiatric medications.

I have rather severe ADHD (attention deficit hyperactivity disorder) Before taking ADHD medications, I would sometimes make impulsive decisions that affected my family, such as blurting out negative comments or making impulsive financial decisions that hurt the family budget.

By taking ADHD medications every day, I can stay focused and organized and do a better job of being a family member and practicing psychiatry with my clients. They also help me write more articles and books.

In my practice of medicine, without these ADHD meds, I could make multiple mistakes, such as leaving dates off prescriptions, losing focus while clients are sharing extremely pertinent data, and so on. Moreover, I write about two or three books every year while on medications and could write only one book every two or three years without them. So if I were too prideful to admit that I had any mental dysfunction, and I refused to take psychiatric medications, I would hinder God, Who gave me that biochemical disability for a reason, using my books, radio talk shows, and TV guest appearances to influence millions of people for His cause. I would be taking the "all natural" route to impress my "new-age" neighbors (and legalistic believers), but accomplish one-third as much for Jesus and for my family.

—PAUL MEIER, M.D.

There is no stigma for people who take thyroid medications for inherited thyroid hormone deficiencies. Millions of diabetics take daily insulin injections giving little thought to the fact that many of them inherited their pancreatic deficiencies. Yet, when it comes to mental health issues many people refuse to accept the notion of inherited abnormalities in brain chemicals. Instead, they suddenly become falsely ashamed and believe they have a character weakness. There is nothing in their lives to cause true guilt, only false guilt.

Are you ashamed when you take aspirin for a headache? Are you ashamed when you take an antibiotic for an infection? No, certainly not! These medications help your body where it is weak, where and when your body does not have enough strength to keep you in good health. Again, the brain is simply one more organ in this imperfect, fallen body God has given us, like the thyroid or pancreas. There is no difference, except in our cultural prejudices.

Some ignorant people will even criticize you for taking a psychiatric medication even though it helps you function better in daily life. Usually people who criticize others the most for taking medicines for the brain are people who have the most brain chemical deficiencies themselves.

When Benjamin Franklin discovered bifocals, some ignorant people called them "devil eyes." In those days, people who wore glasses were often criticized. They were even told by Christian legalists that if they had enough faith in God, He would heal their poor eyesight. This heaped false guilt on people with poor vision whether they wore glasses or not. The same kinds of people today say similar foolish things to people who suffer depression, perfectionism (obsessive-compulsive disorder is severe perfectionism), anxiety, mood swings, schizophrenia, social phobia, paranoia, or even ADHD.

Several years ago, two students at Dallas Theological Seminary became psychotic around the same time. They experienced grandiose and paranoid delusions along with auditory hallucinations (hearing audible voices). They had both inherited schizophrenia, a genetic disorder that affects one percent of the population with symptoms beginning in the late teens or early 20's (though seldom after age 30). Several professors encouraged them to seek treatment in a psychiatric hospital, where both were given medications to correct their dopamine imbalances and restore them to normal within a few weeks, with the help of life-long medication.

One student continued on the medication and fully recovered. He finished seminary, then became a senior pastor at a sizable church and has been quite successful ever since.

The other student grew up in a legalistic church where medications that affected the brain were considered sinful. His pastor visited the hospital and persuaded the young seminarian to discharge early and stop taking medication. The pastor reasoned if this man had enough faith, he would be healed. That student never recovered and continues to be delusional and nonfunctional in society today. He still has the delusion that he is the governor of a large state and hears imaginary voices. His pastor blamed his lack of faith. Shouldn't the blame instead be placed on a pastor who refused to let God work through medication to restore a young man's life?

In the 1990s, an Israeli social worker who was a believer in Yeshua (Jesus), traveled to America for treatment in the Meier Day Program. She suffered from lifelong, severe obsessive compulsive disorder (OCD), which drove her to the point of daily suicidal urges. Still, she loved God and was very faithful in serving Him. She had an underlying genetic disorder involving serotonin. A serotonin antidepressant along with a proper diet resolved her obsessive thoughts and compulsive behaviors allowing her to experience joy and peace for the first time in her life.

When she returned to Israel, her synagogue convinced her that it was wrong to take medications for the brain. They convinced her that even though medications for medical illnesses were fine, psychiatric problems should totally rely on faith and prayer. So she stopped her medications and within a few weeks the obsessive thoughts, compulsive behaviors and daily suicidal urges returned. The synagogue leaders blamed the relapse on her lack of faith. This filled her with intense remorse and guilt. To escape the pain, she committed suicide by hanging herself.

In time, and after being confronted about their attitudes, many members of the congregation at last accepted the notion that mental disorders can be due to factors other than lack of faith. Several members repented of their words and actions toward the social worker. They were good people with good intentions, but they were still living in the dark ages when it came to medical and biblical understanding. Now, that same synagogue uses several of Dr. Meier's books on genetic disorders when they encounter individuals with "blue genes."

When patients refuse psychiatric medications because they have been erroneously taught that all psychiatric problems are spiritual, their lives and those of their families are deeply affected. Consider the examples just presented: The student who humbled himself to take lifelong medication that helps correct his chemical imbalance was able to marry, raise a family, and serve God in an effective, lifelong pastoral ministry. The other seminary student and the Israeli social worker never married, raised children, or served God in an effective way. Both of them most likely would have gone on to live productive and quite normal lives if they had not refused biochemical help.

Most of the people who condemn or criticize others for taking anything "not natural," or for not relying totally on prayer and faith are acting out of ignorance. Clearly it is possible for any believer to live a life of deep faith and devotion while on psychiatric medication. After all, if your car runs out of power-steering fluid, you pull over and pray, but you also call Triple-A (or other help). In the same way, you need to get help when your brain runs out of its power-steering fluid, which is serotonin.

HOPE AND HELP FOR BLUE GENES

Scientific and medical knowledge are exploding in this amazing age of technology, with a doubling rate of five years. Most of the medications we use today were not even on the market five years ago. They offer opportunities for healing that truly reflect God's care and love. Here is just one example of a dramatic life change witnessed at our Meier Day Program:

I was amazed at the miraculous healings that took place using biblical counseling principles and the best new medications. I saw a young college graduate come in who had been both schizophrenic and bipolar all her life and still somehow managed to get through school. All her life, she had paranoid delusions and heard audible voices saying negative things to her.

She couldn't even shop at a grocery store without thinking people were constantly following her down each aisle. She was suicidal almost every day of her life and learned to live in this horrible pain. Dr. Meier and his staff went way out of their way to show her respect and love, and even gave her appropriate hugs for her breakthroughs. Dr. Meier also placed her on a dopamine medication that had only become available that year, along with natural phenylalanine and B6 so her brain would have the raw materials to form the dopamine she so desperately needed in order to gain sanity for the first time in her life.

The new medication helped her brain hang on to the dopamine it was making, and on the eighth day, she went from being a lifelong "insane" person to a normal person, with no delusions, no hallucinations, no anxiety, no paranoia, no depression. In fact, she met herself as a normal person for the first time in her life. All the other clients were amazed as well. I have seen many patients throughout my life, earned three doctorates and written books in France, but I had never seen anything like this in my life, and Dr. Meier's staff does this kind of modern day miracle day in and day out, so routinely that to them it is no harder than changing a flat tire on a car.

—DR. JEAN-LUC BERTRAND

Charles' story from earlier in this chapter also reflects a positive outcome.

After Charles recovered from his lifelong depression, he learned to smile and laugh and was filled with joy. He and his family went on to become missionaries to Ethiopia, where Charles remains today. But Charles did change his plans and ended up going with a supportive mission board, under much less masochistic circumstances than he had originally intended. He would attest to a fulfilling, productive life, filled with love and joy.

If Charles ever quits his antidepressants, he will become as miserable as he was before, but he assures me by e-mail, thirty years later, that he never will. He knows he has inherited blue genes, and he has them well under control. He also has his family and friends high on life's priority list, realizing that as a missionary, he can only give out as much love as he takes in. His life has changed for the better, for the happier.

I love my job! I would rather be a psychiatrist today than to be the President of the United States (although flying around in Air Force One would be nice). The opportunity to help hurting people like Charles change their lives is very rewarding. But it also makes me very sad and angry when I hear of people committing suicide because their well-meaning friends, relatives or pastors laid a guilt trip on them for taking psychiatric medications or for receiving "psychological" counseling.

—PAUL MEIER, M.D.

———

Help is available to all, no matter the cost. The large group of psychiatrists, psychologists and therapists who work at our national, non-profit chain of psychiatric clinics sees over three thousand patients each week. More than 80 percent of patients recover fully with no medications at all, just excellent Christian-based counseling. And God has allowed us to offer over a million dollars in charitable care each year. We are thrilled and awed and thankful to God and the generous Christians who support us.

Through this book we hope to help people understand how genetic makeup affects mental functioning. Our prayer is that it might provide a practical resource, so that if you or one of your family members is suffering from depression or anxiety, you will know where to start.

Inheriting "blue genes" in no way means you cannot and should not live a normal life. The best way to do this is by learning who you truly are, your authentic self. There has never been another you, and the only one who knows you better than you know yourself is God, our Creator, who cares for us so much that He knows the number of hairs on our head. Take this challenge: Educate yourself on your personality! This can be a scary task, because while we find our strengths, we also realize our weaknesses.

Millions of people know only their strengths. Who are they? The arrogant, the un-empathetic, and those who will secretly suffer with a horrible depression or anxiety, because they are too afraid of looking weak if they reach out for help.

Millions of people know only their weaknesses. Who are they? They are the perpetual victims in our society. They spend their time blaming others for their predicament and trying to elicit pity rather than trying to overcome.

When you learn your own strengths and weaknesses, you can then be an educated human instrument of love to the people you love and care about. How? By passing along the amazing information you will discover in this book. Many of our Day Program patients would never have come to the Meier Clinics without being pushed by their families. Depressed people usually want help, but are often too depressed to actually seek it.

Some patients arrive at the urging of a spouse or family member with no intention of learning anything about themselves. Their goal is to try the program just long enough to appease the insistent family member so they can then say, "See, I told you this wouldn't work." To our ongoing amazement—and we give all the glory to God—lives continue to be changed for the better.

Often when a patient leaves the Day Program, a family member or friend will come a few weeks later. They see how this person's whole life has been changed. The patients who complete the three-week program usually have a better understanding of their own bodies, souls, and minds.

After three weeks of spilling their innermost thoughts, feelings and motives with fellow group members in various kinds of group therapy, they generally learn how to develop improved relationships with themselves, with others, and with the real God (not merely the imagined Heavenly version of their earthly fathers as most humans visualize their version of a "god"). These family members, seeing immense changes for the better, now want what this person has.

God wants us to know Him and He wants us to know ourselves (good and bad). You get one life on this earth. Why not live it to the fullest? So many people live the one life God has given them doing exactly what others tell them to do. Parents, spouses, pastors, or best friends all may mean well, but God wants you to search His will for you and make your own decisions.

As you read this book, please keep an open mind. Look for ways God might be speaking to you through this book. Also look for ways God can use you through this book to help someone else who is suffering.

Chapter Two

Serotonin Blue Genes

Edward was a straight-A, pre-law student at Princeton University. He was popular as well as moral and self-disciplined. He was dating another pre-law student he had met in his classes at Princeton. On Christmas Eve of 1998, he proposed to Luci, who promptly accepted. They loved each other deeply.

Edward came from a very warm, loving and intelligent family. He had no significant childhood traumas. He was active socially, succeeding academically, and now was engaged to a wonderful young lady who missed him whenever they were apart.

But Edward had depression that went from feeling almost normal, to almost but not quite suicidal—wishing God would let him die but not planning any methods of self-destruction. He had experienced these depressive dips since early childhood, as had several of his siblings, his mother, and many more of his maternal and paternal relatives.

Edward was a devout Christian, so he prayed often for God to give him some relief, but relief never came for long. When his grades started to go down for the first time in his life, Edward and his parents and Luci all decided that it was time to get Edward some help.

So they flew Edward to Dallas for an evaluation. After asking all my usual questions, I came to the conclusion that Edward had an inherited serotonin problem. People who inherit a low serotonin level have a lifelong dipping of their moods.

They also tend to become more perfectionistic, often counting things obsessively, rechecking doors, hoarding antiques, and developing hand washing rituals because of their compulsive germ phobias. They have a desire to "know everything," so they hoard old newspapers or magazines, intending to read them later without ever actually having time to do so.

They straighten out everyone's pictures, have difficulty getting songs and commercials out of their heads, avoid cracks in the sidewalk, pick at some part of their body or fingernails, or "type words" on their laps.

In the past few months, Edward had recurring bad dreams about being back in high school and not being able to get his locker open. This type of dream is usually an indication that a person grew up with a few too many expectations placed on him, so recurring dreams symbolize failing to please the unpleasable parent. Sometimes these dreams are purely from the genetically low serotonin, driving the person to stay angry with himself for never achieving perfection.

Edward had many genetically depressed relatives. And now Edward was developing more and more sadness, lack of motivation, lack of energy, excessive false guilt, insomnia, increased irritability, painful thinking, a desire to withdraw from people, and a loss of interest in doing the things he once enjoyed with Luci.

He had more and more death wishes, and sometimes had panic attacks that felt as though he were going to go crazy. Two of his cousins had actually become schizophrenic, a lifelong genetic illness marked by delusions and hallucinations that can be corrected (but not cured) by taking dopamine-correcting medication.

Some people have panic attacks and feel like they are going crazy when in reality they are not even close to losing touch. It is just an unrealistic fear. On the other hand, some people develop these panic attacks and feel like they are going to "go crazy" soon. And in their case, they are actually insightful. They are going to lose their ability to comprehend reality soon, unless they get on dopamine medications to prevent it.

We did psychological testing on Edward to see what the computer guessed Edward was really like. His testing showed that he was close to psychosis. If this had happened to Edward sixty or seventy years ago, he likely would have lost touch with reality, stayed that way, and spent the rest of his life in a mental hospital, thinking he had special powers and becoming a threat to himself and others.

—Paul Meier, M.D.

The Serotonin Solution

Serotonin is the brain amine which is probably the most influential chemical in our bodies. Edward's problems illustrate what can happen when this chemical is out of balance and too low. If each of us is basically as happy as our brain's serotonin level, what can we do to help our family and friends keep their levels up? The answer to that life-changing question is the focus of this chapter.

What is serotonin? You can't eat and digest serotonin, and it can't be injected. God created us in such a way that only our own brain can make serotonin to float in the synapses (spaces) between our 40 billion brain and nerve cells. Our brain and nerve cells also have reuptake sites that draw the serotonin back up, to keep it in proper balance.

If you have the right amount of serotonin in your brain cell synapses, you are filled with love, joy, peace, long-suffering, gentleness, meekness, energy during the day, great sleep at night, and so on. Separate areas of your brain control these different behaviors. Serotonin is one of four key brain amines that work together to regulate our behavior. For clarity, we should take a brief look at the other three, which will crop up frequently in this book.

Another important brain amine that our brain produces is *dopamine,* which gives us sanity. If your dopamine levels went out of balance for any reason right now, you would immediately start thinking you heard negative voices saying nasty things to you outside your head. You might look around to see who was speaking to you, and nobody else would be in the room, which would be very frightening. Likely you would erroneously assume that it must be God, or an angel, or a demon, or some sort of ghost.

You would also immediately have more difficulty holding thoughts together (thought-blocking). You would also become paranoid, and probably think someone was out to get you. You might become grandiose, thinking that you were God or at least His right-hand assistant. Different dopamine medications must be used for different dopamine problems— whether too much or too little.

There is another chemical in our brain called *GABA (gamma-amino-butyric-acid),* which puts the brakes on our worries, takes away our shyness, helps with sleep, decreases physical pain, takes away drug and alcohol cravings, and helps us to have muscle relaxation. Psychiatrists are now using some of the GABA medications to treat bipolar mood swings. GABA medications (i.e., Depakote-ER, Gabitril, Keppra, Topamax, Neurontin, etc.) not only improve mood swings in bipolar disorder, but they also decrease alcohol and many drug cravings. This new medical approach, along with programs like Celebrate Recovery and Alcoholics Anonymous, will hopefully meet with increased success in the future in reducing alcoholism. Lamictal also works very well for both mania and depression and also works like a GABA medicine, but its total mechanisms of action are not known at the time of this printing.

So far we have discussed three brain amines: serotonin, dopamine and GABA. *Norepinephrine,* a fourth brain amine, is the brain's version of adrenaline. It mediates energy, motivation, sexual pleasure and improved mental focus. Low norepinephrine levels lead to sexual dysfunction, chronic fatigue, forgetfulness, lack of motivation and depression. This is one reason why depressed people have unusually low energy and sexual desire. Norepinephrine levels that are too high result in anxiety, insomnia, and even panic attacks.

As you can see, if these four brain amines are all working in balance, we feel better and enjoy life more, regardless of circumstances. At the Meier Clinics, the goal is to balance serotonin, dopamine, GABA and norepinephrine, usually by learning and practicing spiritual attitudes and behaviors.

Sometimes medications are needed either short term or long term. For instance, of the approximately three thousand patients seen each week at the Meier Clinics, about 80 percent of these patients can manage this chemical balance without medications, just by living according to Scriptural principles and eating the right amount of three essential amino acids in our diets: tryptophan, phenylalanine, tyrosine and another essential nutrient, choline.

TREATMENT FOR EDWARD

When I considered Edward's medications, I decided to treat not only Edward but also his entire family tree. My goal was to correct Edward's brain chemistry as quickly as possible, so he would feel great and relaxed.

I gave him Effexor-XR, one of the most powerful antidepressants, along with Wellbutrin-XL, a norepinephrine/dopamine antidepressant that enhances any of the serotonin antidepressants and provides lots of energy, improved focus and a more enjoyable physical relationship in marriage.

I also added two dopamine medications. Some psych meds make people gain thirty or forty pounds. Other psych meds cause an average of a twenty-pound weight loss. Edward was about six-foot-four and 260 pounds. In my experience, Effexor and Wellbutrin each cause about a five pound weight loss, Risperdal and Seroquel both tend to add five or ten pounds; I knew they would work well to relieve Edward's symptoms.

Edward was engaged by now, and he expressed concern about three things with the wedding coming up in four months: First, he wanted me to get rid of his painful and frequent panic attacks. Second, he didn't want any of the meds to wipe out his ability to have sex, since his honeymoon was coming up soon. Third, he didn't want his wife to begin their marriage with a depressed husband.

So I explained to him that the Effexor-XR should decrease or eliminate his panic attacks within ten weeks; it takes that long for the serotonin to build back up, even with the medications. I handed Edward a handful of Klonopin wafers samples and wrote him a perscription for more, and explained that the Klonopin wafers are a very safe and powerful minor tranquilizer. They dissolve in your mouth within a few seconds, and eliminate a panic attack within four minutes, keeping anxiety away for eight hours. There are a large number of GABA medications, like Klonopin wafers, and all of them help anxiety, help take away drug and alcohol cravings, and decrease physical pain.

If Edward felt panicky, he should peel out the wafer, suck on it like a communion wafer, dissolving it in about two seconds, and within four minutes his panic attack would be completely gone. The wafer keeps anxiety away for eight hours.

Edward's psychological testing showed that his fears of "going crazy" were realistic fears. He was close to losing touch with reality, like a couple of his cousins had. That is why I added two dopamine medications, which work just like "ego glue" to hold the thinking together. People in psychosis have thought blocking, where they lose their train of thought in the middle of a sentence and forget what they are talking about. It is almost impossible to "go crazy" while faithfully taking a dopamine medicine.

With the wedding coming up, Edward was also concerned about whether the meds would make him impotent or fat. I explained to him that the Wellbutrin-XL enhances sexual enjoyment as well as enhancing the effects of the other meds.

Edward did well on the meds and improved nutrition, got lots of counseling, and within ten weeks his depressive affect and panic attacks were completely gone. He used Klonopin wafers during that transition and never had another panic attack the rest of his life, as I had told him to expect.

I assured Edward and Luci that they should be about to have a normal life, a normal or better than normal career. Edward and Luci went on their honeymoon and just had a great time. He also lost 20 pounds and looked great, though not as great as he said Luci did to him that day.

A decade later I still follow Edward for his med checks four times a year. On the meds, Edward has had a steady life, graduating from a prestigious law school, along with his wife, then joining a Christian law firm together in Atlanta, Georgia. Luci went to a part-time law practice when their son, Edward Jr., was born.

—Paul Meier, M.D.

Beyond Medications

Medications were of great help in Edward's case. But nutrition and counseling also have a big impact in treatment. So then how can we help our family members and friends to get those four essential nutrients from the dinner table (bananas, broccoli, nuts, meats, dairy products, leafy green vegetables, etc.) to the stomach, then to the bloodstream, then past the blood-brain barrier into their brains, and then to work correctly within their brains?

Well, believe it or not, the most important factors are spiritual, especially in the way we handle anger. If we hold within us enough pent-up anger, the reuptake sites in our brain cells work overtime to draw the serotonin out of the synapses (spaces) between our brain cells. Serotonin is implicated in the cause of many types of headaches, including migraines.

Now if the brain is too low in serotonin, we become depressed, unloving, anxious, impatient, more fatigued, more withdrawn, more guilt-ridden, more "pained," less gentle, irritable, less able to practice self-control, and more likely to keep waking up at night, especially at about three in the morning.

Ephesians 4:26-27 tells us it is fine to get angry, without sinning, if we get rid of the anger by bedtime. Holding on to the anger gives Satan a foothold in our lives. We know from science that people who hold grudges experience more depression and (you guessed it) lower brain serotonin levels. So quite a bit of insomnia and probably most depression is caused by holding on to our anger, rather than expressing it and letting it go.

Psychiatrists realized over a hundred years ago, before we ever even knew that serotonin existed, that "anger turned inward" is a huge reason for depression and other illnesses. Bitterness toward self, God, or others releases ACTH-RF (adrenocorticotrophic hormone releasing factor) from the hypothalamus. This in turn causes the pituitary to release ACTH (adrenocorticotrophic hormone), causing the adrenals to release too many stress hormones, causing our white blood cells to produce fewer antibodies to fight off diseases, which can result in illnesses and death.

Romans 6:23 says that the wages for our sins is death. This verse has spiritual (spiritual death) as well as physical implications. If you go to an emergency room with a migraine, what do they do? They give you a shot of Imitrex, which simply blocks the serotonin receptors in the blood vessels so you won't get the headache God may have intended for you to get for disobeying Ephesians 4:26-27 and holding a grudge.

Really nice people often get migraines too, so why is that? It is because "really nice people" tend to be people pleasers. They allow selfish people to take advantage of them. They think they "can't say no." Except that there is no such thing as "can't," just "won't." The truth is, really nice people "won't" say no, because they are so afraid of confrontation or rejection. They felt rejected and conditionally accepted by a demanding parent growing up, in most cases, so they continue to think externally. They find their self-esteem in the eyes of others, especially their parents.

God declares you to be a person of high esteem in Psalm 139 and many other places. If you become more spiritually mature, you will accept God's wonderful opinion of you. And God declares you significant to Him knowing full well all your past, present and future sins. You will never surprise God. Our worth and His love are unconditional.

When you mature spiritually, you will become more of an "internal thinker" rather than an externalizer. You will be able to say to yourself, "God loves and accepts me. I love and accept me. My parents are only two out of six billion people on this planet. I do not need their acceptance any more than I need anyone else's acceptance."

Psalm 68 tells us that God takes the lonely and places them in families. He will help you find better friends who will not take advantage of you. Make these better friends your new family. This is the family of God. These are your brothers and sisters.

That is what Jesus was trying to tell His disciples (and us) over and over again. When Jesus was fellowshipping with people He loved, some of His disciples started to criticize Him, because His mother, Mary, was waiting for Him outside. They thought He should rush to her, since she was His parent.

Do you remember what He told them? He looked around the room at the good people He was fellowshipping with and said that *these* were His mother, and father, and brothers and sisters.

Unlike Jesus, we try to please our parents too much at times, even when they are being selfish. Of course we must honor out parents, but some abusive parents must be avoided, even while we help them in ways that are not enabling. Then we go through life trying to please other selfish people who remind us of our parents unconsciously. Then they use and abuse us. Then we get angry with these narcissists.

The trouble is that these nice people fool themselves into thinking they are not angry at the jerks, stuffing their anger, holding unconscious grudges that they may become aware of, or may refuse to acknowledge. All of this causes their reuptake sites to draw up serotonin and causes their stress hormones to suppress antibodies, and the cycle goes on. That is the way God built us.

By the way, what is happening whenever you keep feeling guilty? If you stop to think about it, we have true guilt, for things we have done that hurt people. (God doesn't call anything a sin unless it hurts someone, so when He asks you to quit sinning, He is simply encouraging you to love and be loved more by not hurting people, including a very important person to Him—His own son or daughter—you!)

He is not trying to deprive you of fun. He is telling you not to hold grudges and get vengeance on people. We all need to learn to say yes when yes is appropriate, and to say no when no is appropriate, then let the chips fall wherever they fall. If narcissistic people reject us for not allowing them to further abuse us, then thank God for losing those people. God has lovingly delivered you.

God has taken the weeds out of your garden. Don't cry because you miss those weeds. When you say no to their selfish demands, you are making God happy. The "guilt" you feel is only false guilt.

And what is true guilt then? It is anger again—but anger at yourself for hurting someone. And do we have a right to stay angry with ourselves when we do horrible things?

No we don't! Jesus died on the cross to pay for all our sins. You were already forgiven before you even sinned if you have asked Jesus into your life. Romans 8:1 tells us that there is absolutely no condemnation for those who belong to Jesus. When you hold a grudge against yourself for past sins, that grudge is a worse sin than whatever sin you committed in the first place.

You are playing God, by holding vengeful motives toward yourself. He forgives you, so He wants you to get off your own back and accept His grace. If you don't forgive yourself, you will drain your brain of serotonin and start ACTH-RF rolling out of your hypothalamus and the whole cycle begins once more. And it can end in your own death if you let it.

And what is another example of false guilt? A good example of false guilt is an innocent little girl who has a very evil father who selfishly uses her as a sexual object to make himself feel more important. It is not her fault, but she thinks it is. She thinks she is trash, but she is not trash; she is God's eternal daughter. So if she never gets professional counseling, she may never realize that she is innocent, she is not trash, she does not deserve punishment.

She deserves to love herself and become her own best friend. But if she never sees the truth, the truth will not set her free from her anger toward herself, anger that turns on the reuptake sites for serotonin and begins the series of chain reactions we described earlier.

As we said before, most people can correct low levels of these four vital amines in their brains by forgiving and obeying the "one-another" concepts in Scripture. We obey these (and obey God) when we confront one another, speak the truth in love, rebuke one another, love one another, weep with those who weep, and confess our faults to each other (see James 5:16).

People come from around the world to our Day Program in Dallas— from Israel, Saudi Arabia, Europe, South America, Asia, Africa, and elsewhere. Then we put them into small groups of clients with a trained Christian therapist in each small group, and they confess their faults and hurts to each other until the tears are all gone.

Then they are healed. We try to get our clients to cry, because Jesus said that He would bless those who mourn by finally feeling comfort (the beatitudes, Matthew chapter 5, etc.). Our clinics have grown over the years because we have seen the results of simply teaching people how to put God's biblical instructions into practice. God deserves the credit because He is the one who heals them, but God has provided us with gifted, loving therapists. They are spiritually astute enough to think of innovative ways to teach people how to actually apply, rather than just learn, God's healing principles.

The Meier Clinics have been around for almost 30 years now, and the Holy Spirit has led over a million people to trust Christ as a result of various Meier Clinic-related ministries (through therapy, seminars, books, radio, TV, training, mission trips, etc.). About a third of our clientele are nonbelievers when they start therapy. We even had a topless dancer check into our Day Program recently because we were on her insurance provider list. She became a believer and learned how to really love and be loved.

I saw a new patient this very morning who began having panic attacks a few months ago. He has two sisters with schizophrenia, a genetic dopamine problem. So when he told me during a painful panic attack right there in my office that he could barely hang onto his sanity, I believed him.

I reassured him that within five minutes his panic attack would be over, and within an hour the threat of losing touch with reality would be taken care of. My nurse, Lynne, and I immediately gave him a Klonopin wafer, which eliminated the panic attack in four minutes.

Then we gave him an Abilify tablet (a dopamine-regulating, atypical antipsychotic agent), and within an hour his thinking slowed down and he relaxed even more. He knew he was on the road to recovery. He checked into our Day Program, where Dr. Clements and I can monitor his meds and his progress daily, and where our therapists can find out what stressors caused him to become psychotically depressed in the first place.

This is a good example of someone who has spiritual and emotional problems to resolve. He shared with us this morning a number of things that he was bitter about. His bitterness caused a serotonin depletion. He himself did not have schizophrenia, but because two sisters did, he had those "blue genes" tendencies, and tipped over the edge.

He heard voices that morning that were not really there, and he was getting mildly delusional.

But after one day on these modern meds, he is much better already. Three weeks of therapy and medication adjustment will make him stronger than he ever was before.

—Paul Meier, M.D.

The Promise of Help

The previous story is a perfect example of how counseling and medication can combine to offer hope and help for "blue genes" issues. Up to half of the American population has an inherited predisposition for some mental abnormality (depression, bipolar, schizophrenia, OCD, etc.). With the medications we have today, these people can lead normal lives. In ten years, the treatments available will by far exceed those of today, so the future looks bright.

My own family (Meier) has a history of mild depressions (dysthymia) and ADHD (bored easily, impulsive, forgetful, daydream a lot, etc.). My 96-year-old mother, for example, does great on a certain type of antidepressant that keeps her serotonin level in a normal range.

I have better results (for me) on another type of antidepressant that keeps my norepinephrine balanced, which improves my ADHD. In my opinion, it would be wrong for me to refuse to take medications that render me much more useful to the cause of Christ.

If you have suffered with depression or another mental illness you certainly may have underlying genetic influences or "blue genes." Taking a family history is very helpful. Do any of your parents or siblings have any psychiatric problems? Find out about cousins, aunts, and uncles as well.

When it comes to grandparents, they may have had a psychiatric condition that was never diagnosed. It is important to find out from other family members if they exhibited strange behavior or had alcohol or drug problems.

Those with "blue genes" do better mentally, physically and spiritually with medication. We see many of these people in our clinic who refuse psychiatric medication until they finally feel so bad, or life is so out of control, that they can't take it anymore. They begrudgingly start on medication, but when they feel better they stop, and often insist they really didn't need it in the first place. They may do fine for a while, but the problem invariably returns and we go through the whole ordeal again. Interestingly, this group of people often has no problem whatsoever when it comes to taking medicine for conditions such as high blood pressure, diabetes, or arthritis.

What's so different about mental illness? The brain is an organ that can have problems just like any other organ. People have no problem believing they inherited epilepsy or migraine headaches when they see other family members with the same condition. You would be hard pressed to find a migraine sufferer who refuses medications that will help. Migraines are located in the brain just like depression and bipolar. They are often inherited just like depression and bipolar. Why do we deal with them so differently?

To end this chapter on a positive note, there is good news for a lot of readers who only have a mild serotonin problem: chronic mild dysthymia. With this condition most people function adequately, but they nearly always feel just a little sadder than their friends.

If this were a genetic serotonin problem, these clients would be encouraged to take a lifelong serotonin medicine, such as Zoloft, Lexapro, Effexor-XR, or Cymbalta. Most of these clients continue to feel just fine on one of these medications for many years.

Cynthia Pauling, for example, has been coming to the clinic for a fifteen-minute medicine check every three months for fourteen years now. She has a genetic serotonin problem and was mildly to moderately depressed since birth, until she began taking Prozac fourteen years ago, as a seventeen-year-old high school junior.

She has felt great ever since, and we only changed her medicine once, when she noticed sexual side effects for the first time on her honeymoon at age 22. Now, at age 31, she has two children and is helping her husband, Jack, run his own trucking supply company out of their home.

Chapter Three

Blue Genes, Sleep and Dreams

"My son, preserve sound judgment and discernment, do not let them out of your sight; they will be life for you, an ornament to grace your neck. Then you will go on your way in safety, and your foot will not stumble; when you lie down, you will not be afraid; when you lie down, your sleep will be sweet."

—PROVERBS 3:21-24

Jennifer was a professional woman who checked herself into our Day Program a few years ago complaining of seven straight years of sadness with periods of suicidal urges. During the worst times of her depression she woke up every morning around three o'clock and usually could not fall asleep for at least two hours. This lady, described by friends as a hard worker with a brilliant mind, could now barely function at her job due to fatigue.

Questions about her life revealed a happy, normal childhood. She insisted there were no current life crises. She could not recall any family members who had ever suffered from depression. There was no evidence of genetic or "familial" depression.

I asked her to recall the events of that summer seven years ago when her depression originally began. Again, nothing in particular came to mind. As I continued taking a detailed history, an interesting pattern emerged. Her depression and insomnia worsened every summer, which is usually a happy time for people.

I felt there must be some repressed event in her life that took place in the summer seven years earlier which now made her unconsciously angry with herself, God or someone else. Yet even with the help of our trained therapists she could not recall any upsetting or traumatic event happening that summer.

Halfway through the second week of the program I became frustrated and concerned that we might not be able to assist this wonderful young woman. She still struggled with urges to kill herself and was quickly becoming more desperate as therapy was not helping.

On her daily rounds to visit with me, I told her how frustrated I was that we had not been able to dig up the root cause (or causes) of her depression, which we usually do the first week. I would have to take an unusual approach with Jennifer in order to help her with her sleep problems.

—PAUL MEIER, M.D.

——————

Mark Twain once said, "It's not what you eat that gives you indigestion, it's what's eating you." The same could be said for insomnia. It's not usually what you eat that keeps you awake (although it could be), but what is "eating you." This was certainly true in Jennifer's case.

The causes of insomnia are many and varied—many of them directly tied to "blue genes." Anxiety is the leading cause; it creates fragmented sleep due to frequent awakenings. During her wakeful periods, Jennifer had a hard time shutting down her brain as it resumed worrying repeatedly.

Depression often causes insomnia and alters a person's normal 90-minute sleep cycle. Normally dreaming (called REM sleep) lasts around 20 minutes of a cycle. Non-REM sleep refreshes and repairs the physical body while REM sleep repairs the mind. When a person is depressed, REM sleep is increased, as if the mind is working overtime to repair itself.

Depression also causes a sleep abnormality known as early-morning awakenings, when a person wakes up 2–3 hours before the alarm clock goes off and then cannot fall back to sleep. For many people this is the most painful part of depression. The mind will not stop focusing on negative thoughts, and people are consumed with negative thoughts about themselves, their lives and the world in general. The future looks hopeless as well.

Serotonin is the main neurochemical that helps us sleep well and feel rested the next day. When it is low or out of balance in the brain, it not only leads to depression, but poor sleep. In fact, poor sleep may be one of the main reasons for the depression rather than vice versa. One study found that depressed people reported poor sleep as the first sign they were heading into another depressive episode.

Repressed anger (at God, at others, or at self either for actual guilt or false guilt) is another issue that leads to depression and/or loss of sleep. Your thoughts really do have power. Good thoughts bring peace and comfort. Negative thoughts bring agitation, anxiety and eventually depression. Thoughts of anger are very powerful both physically and mentally. If you doubt that, take a moment to remember how your body reacts when you get angry.

Emotions and thoughts play a large role in modifying the chemistry of our brains. As Jennifer discovered, buried feelings related to the past can cause depression and sleep disorders as well.

As I worked to find an answer to help Jennifer, I asked if I could pray with her for insight. So I prayed that God would give us a breakthrough and discover Jennifer's root problem, so she could recover from her depression.

I felt led to pray that Jennifer would have a dream that night that would give us a clue into the root problem, so I did pray that. After the prayer, I told Jennifer I really hoped she would have that dream.

That night I had a very intense dream concerning Jennifer. Jesus was in my dream, and He looked at Jennifer, then at me, and told me specifically to ask her about an abortion. I reassured Jesus that she had told me she never had an abortion, but He just looked at me in a loving, nonjudgmental way that seemed to convey a message of "trust Me."

I am a very skeptical psychiatrist, so I never know for sure whether a dream I have is really from God, or just caused by eating jalapenos at a Mexican restaurant the night before. But this one felt like a real "God dream" to me. I knew that whatever Jennifer had dreamed that night, I still had a moral obligation to ask her again about an abortion. I feared offending her since I had already asked and she clearly told me no.

When I asked if she recalled any dreams from the night before, she said no in a disappointed tone. I told her about my dream, assuring her that I did not know for certain whether my dream came from God or from indigestion! She was quite stunned, and replied matter-of-factly, "Well, actually, I did have one abortion but it didn't bother me in the least because I am pro-abortion, and I know it was the proper thing for me to do under the circumstances."

I assured her that I had no desire to argue with her about "pro" or "anti" abortion issues, but that I just wanted to help relieve her pain because of my compassion for her. I asked when she had the abortion.

She hesitated for what seemed like an eternity, then finally blurted out, "During the summer, seven years ago. But I'm sure this depression doesn't have anything to do with that abortion. It's all just a coincidence."

One way psychiatrists often pull repressed emotions to the surface is by using what is called a "Gestalt technique," which includes such things as talking to an empty chair while envisioning your abuser sitting there, or writing a letter to someone who hurt you and expressing the feelings you've always held inside. This helps even if you don't mail the letter. I suggested this approach to Jennifer.

Jennifer quickly agreed she would be more than willing to write a letter to her aborted baby. I asked her to decide whether the aborted baby was a boy or a girl and to assume the baby was an adult in heaven, having a great time while looking forward to the day he or she would get to meet Jennifer. She would name the child, then write a personal letter to him or her, explaining her feelings.

When I asked her if she would read the letter to me when finished, she replied, "No problem." She felt I was barking up the wrong tree and agreed to do it just to get me off her back.

That night, alone in her motel room, Jennifer named her son and started writing him a letter. Halfway through the letter, seven years of buried emotions came gushing out of her like a volcano (a phenomenon psychiatrists call "decathexis," whereby emotions that are buried in the unconscious flood to the surface).

She wept for several hours a day for the next three or four days over her regret at ending a human life—her own flesh and blood. Then she prayed for God's forgiveness and chose to forgive herself for the decision she made seven summers ago.

Her depression almost immediately dissipated for the first time in seven years. She sleeps "like a baby" now and reports pleasant dreams, just as wise King Solomon promised three thousand years ago if we gain insight (Proverbs 3:21).

Jesus promised that if we learn the truth, it will set us free, and when Jennifer learned the truth about her suppressed shame and grief and got it out in the open, the truth set her free.

Removing her emotional "post-abortion-syndrome" block helped her to quit isolating herself, and when she became active in a local church, she met a great guy and married him a year later. Recently she gave birth to a beautiful baby girl. Jennifer will make a great wife and mother now, and a great friend to herself. She knows that some day her new daughter, Tiffany, will meet her older, aborted sibling in heaven. Jennifer's note to me recently says she is really at peace with it now.

—PAUL MEIER, M.D.

THE POWER OF DREAMS

Jennifer's breakthrough was a result of several key elements, including the power of dreams to communicate.

A few thousand years ago King David wrote that God guides us in various ways not only during the daytime, but also during the nights: "Even at night my heart instructs me," (Psalm 16:7). There are 150 passages of Scripture that address dreams. Dreams have always served as an important part of God's communion with people; for example, God spoke to Jacob, Daniel, Mother Mary, Joseph, and a host of other biblical characters in dreams.

The more anxious and/or depressed we are, the lower our serotonin level, and the worse our dreams become. For instance, we may dream of tornadoes, being chased, trying to get somewhere without finding our way, or taking a test and not being able to finish it. We can have dreams of falling (showing that we're afraid of failing at something), dreams with teeth missing or some other facial disfigurement (a fear of "losing face"), and dreams where we're getting hurt or even dying or exacting revenge on others.

Dreams are a revealing and helpful tool for treating some disorders brought about by blue genes and other causes—so much so that patients at the Meier Day Program in Dallas, Texas are regularly asked about their dreams. Patients usually start dreaming more when they come to the Day Program than they did previously, and these dreams are often more vivid as well. No doubt this is due to the seven hours a day they spend in educational, spiritual, and interactive group therapy. During group and individual therapy our counselors probe and dig to help each patient discover where the root of his or her problem lies. Patients learn how to remember their dreams so they can report them in detail. This is very helpful in revealing to me the root of their current problems, as it was in the case of "Michigan Molly."

Molly was one of the most popular young women in America. Not only was she a state champion gymnast, she had gone on to win two gold medals in the Olympics. She made millions of dollars on advertising endorsements. She had parents, siblings, friends, and even a wonderful boyfriend who all adored her. She was a committed Christian and was very sweet and beautiful. She even had a ministry, planning to devote her life to help train future Olympic gymnasts and help them develop a deep relationship with God at the same time.

But Molly had horrific nightmares almost every night. In these dreams, she was usually in the backseat of her mother's car, with her mother driving. They would hit a patch of Michigan ice and crash into a church building. The car burst into flames and they both died.

For months Molly woke up with panic attacks, weeping. She was suicidal as well. Her agonizing pain came from two sources: blue genes and a root emotional problem. Molly was a bulimic. In spite of staying thin and beautiful, short little Michigan Molly binge ate over 15,000 calories a day, and had no power whatsoever to stop doing so. She also vomited on purpose from four to eight times a day, and had no power whatsoever to stop doing so.

Blue genes affected Molly with an inherited low serotonin level, resulting in chronic mild dysthymia (sadness) that occasionally dipped into suicidal depressions. The low serotonin also caused Molly to be a perfectionist, which was both a blessing and a curse.

Her perfectionism drove her to excel in grades, in sports, and in almost every other area of her life. But her perfectionism also caused her to count things compulsively everywhere she went, to wash her already sore hands compulsively, and to become furious at herself every time she made any mistake. She actually hated herself for being so imperfect. But she could put on the brightest smile to cover up the truth from her friends and relatives.

Michigan Molly also had a root emotional problem—a problem so painful that she binge ate to medicate herself and vomited compulsively rid herself of that painful aspect of her life. The most common root problem in bulimia (a disorder affecting primarily young women who compulsively vomit or abuse laxatives for weight control) is over-enmeshment with their mothers, women who are so dependent on the young daughters that they want to be "best friends," calling on the phone for an hour or more every single day. And Molly was no exception to the rule.

Since Molly's mom and dad lacked emotional intimacy, Mom was very lonely and invested her whole life in Molly. Molly became Mom's best friend, and though Mom meant well, she thought too much for Molly and made too many of Molly's decisions. Molly became passive, dependent, and an externalizer, thinking her entire self-worth came from what her mother thought of her.

Molly was afraid to think for herself, because she knew deep down that this would hurt her mother's feelings, as if Mom wasn't necessary any more. If Molly individuated and became her own person, Mom would fall apart and get suicidal, and Molly thought that would mean she had killed her mother.

Molly had a horrible dilemma: Should she become independent, make the break from her mom, develop her own friends, and go to the college of her choice? Was she really free to choose her church, spend time with friends, or marry? Or must she let her mother make all her decisions and control her life?

Unable to face this painful dilemma that could kill her mother via suicide, and plagued by compounding blue genes that contributed to her compulsions and depression, Molly made food a substitute for true unconditional love, binge eating and vomiting repeatedly without understanding the causes.

Her recurrent dreams about being in the backseat of her mother's car reflected the fact that her mother was driving Molly's life. They crashed into a church because Molly felt falsely guilty for wanting to break free from Mom, knowing that doing so might result in Mom committing suicide. In the nightmares, Mom and Molly both die, because as long as they stay overly enmeshed with each other, death is where they are both headed.

When Molly's mother brought her to Dallas for treatment in the Meier Day Program, the problem was clear: Molly, a gold medalist in her early twenties, was totally controlled by her mom, who even answered for her daughter when Molly was asked medical questions in the psychiatric evaluation.

Over a three week period, Molly had to come to grips with her relationship with her mother and understand her false guilt and behaviors prompted by her blue genes. As she began to get well, her dreams also "got well." By the time Molly went home from the Day Program, she was having dreams in which she was driving her own car, or even flying airplanes, with friends beside her.

HOW DREAMS WORK

Sixty percent of Americans sleep just fine and report pleasant dreams a majority of the time. Everyone dreams twenty minutes or so during a normal sleep cycle of ninety minutes. Dreams can only be remembered if the person awakens while the dream is occurring. Rapid Eye Movement (REM) is the phase of sleep when most dreaming occurs.

During REM sleep our eyes remain closed, but are moving back and forth rapidly under the lids. Most of our muscles are paralyzed (scientists believe this keeps us from acting out our dreams), but sleep talking and sleep walking are common and normal. How do we know what goes on during sleep? Physicians can study sleep by connecting a patient to an EEG machine. Each sleep phase emits a distinct electrical brain wave pattern.

How often have you experienced an insightful dream, then told your-self in the middle of the night, "I can't wait to share this with my mate or pastor or therapist"? Then when you awaken the next morning, you remember having an important dream but can't recall more than bits or pieces. Part of you wants to know more about your soul, but a large part of you is scared the truth will hurt. Your brain frequently builds dreams around painful issues that you are unwilling to recognize or resolve. Often a person is unaware of how suppressed conscious emotions resurface in the sub-consciousness of dreams.

NIGHTMARES

When we are happy and at peace and have normal serotonin levels, we dream about flying (succeeding or connecting in positive ways with others or of helping others). We have dreams of loving and being loved. But what about scary dreams, bad dreams that often plague the sleep of children?

Children may have nightmares stemming from stress in their lives—seeing Mom and Dad argue or other family conflicts, or getting bullied by older siblings or by bullies at school. Children who are sexually abused can also have post-traumatic stress reaction, which nearly always causes nightmares.

If your child has nightmares, take time to listen and try to figure out what he or she really fears. Then send the child back to his or own bed. Children older than three should not sleep with a parent except on very rare occasions.

Night terrors are different and are common in two to four percent of young children. They run in families and are most likely genetically related (one of our many possible "blue genes"). The child appears awake as he screams and thrashes around. Trying to awaken him can make things worse, and a parent might get injured. Usually it's best to just try to pro-tect him from being hurt. Hold him if he allows you to, but protect him from self-harm if he won't.

If the night terrors continue, a pediatrician or child psychiatrist can prescribe medication, which will usually diminish them. Medications will also help with bedwetting, tics, perfectionism, depression, anger outbursts, and many other problems. Medication helps rebalance serotonin levels, which may be off as the result of genetic serotonin depletion, or may be off because of anger, guilt, stress, or other factors as well.

Parents should be sure their children engage in a positive activity before they go to bed. A "spooky" movie or scary video game right before bed can translate into nightmares that night, even if everything is going well in their lives. Children often have difficulty separating fantasy from reality.

SEROTONIN AND SLEEP

A classic symptom of low serotonin and clinical depression is waking up at three o'clock in the morning. People can only sleep well with adequate serotonin. And we cannot dream without serotonin either. In our opinion, serotonin is the most important chemical in our bodies.

Without adequate serotonin in our brains, we cannot even experience love, joy, peace, patience, gentleness, meekness, humility, self-control—the fruit of the Spirit. People who inherit normal brain chemicals (80 percent of the population), and also practice the behaviors, thinking, and sharing of emotions and confessing of faults as instructed in the Bible, have joyful, meaningful lives with the fruit of the Spirit.

People who inherit normal brain chemicals but disobey God's loving recommendations for us by becoming bitter, negative, controlling, secretive, dishonest, etc., will become serotonin-depleted and become clinically depressed. What seems unfair to me is that there are millions of wonderful people who do all the right things and still feel like killing themselves, and many do, because they inherited low serotonin levels and never took medication to correct this imbalance. On serotonin medications, they are as happy as a lark.

In summary: happy people dream happy dreams. Depressed patients often report nightmares and negative dreams. As their depression and anxiety improve, the content of their dreams also improves. Depression and anxiety have major effects on the quantity and quality of sleep. Genetic factors and blue genes play an important role in sleep, and can contribute to insomnia, nightmares, night terrors, and nighttime panic attacks. A more detailed list of these factors follows.

Genetic depression or chronic mild dysthymia results in a person feeling somewhat sadder than peers throughout life because of abnormally low serotonin activity in areas of the brain that control emotions (i.e., the limbic system). Major depression happens in cycles, and the person usually feels normal between episodes. Dysthymia is more of a low-grade depression that is persistent for at least two years. These people often have a negative pessimistic attitude. A person with both dysthymia and major depression is said to have "double depression." Physicians find dysthymia more difficult to treat than major depression, but nearly 100 percent of depressions can be helped.

S.A.D.—Seasonal Affective Disorder—is a good example of a genetic depression that is affected by the environment in combination with the hormone melatonin. People with S.A.D. have depressive episodes during the winter, when the amount of daylight is lowest. During the summer they usually feel fine. This is because melatonin, which keeps sleep cycles regular, is produced more abundantly in winter due to longer hours of darkness. A small percentage of the population releases too much melatonin. This results in decreased serotonin in the part of the brain that regulates mood and sleep.

S.A.D. occurs at a higher rate in the northern states, due to diminished winter sunlight compared to the south. Many people with S.A.D. can move south and not suffer with depression during the winter, thanks to increased exposure to bright sunshine. Yet even a move southward fails to help some. These people have a blue gene that signals the brain to release too much serotonin. In this case, S.A.D. can be treated with either serotonin antidepressants or a 10,000 lumen lamp 30 minutes a day or more (or both in some cases).

A 10,000 lumen light can be purchased from a number of sources. A person can read or watch TV sitting next to it for at least 30 minutes a day during the winter to prevent depression. You can visit WebMD.com and search for Seasonal Affective Disorder for more information.

Bipolar spectrum disorders affect people who inherit mood swings. This condition was formerly known as "manic-depressive illness," but is now called cyclothymia or bipolar I or bipolar II (the milder form of bipolar). People who inherit cyclothymia or bipolar disorder (about five percent of the adult population) usually experience insomnia during the "highs." Some bipolar patients complain of insomnia all the time regardless of their mood.

These patients are usually caught in a quandary. They often require long-term sleep aid medications. Yet most sleeping medications bought over the counter (OTC) affect sleep architecture, so even though the person may sleep several hours, he or she does not feel nearly as rested. Most OTC sleep medications leave morning "hangovers" as well. Patients may have to take something stimulating (like caffeine) just to wake up. Almost all OTC sleep aids are antihistamines, which stimulate appetite and promote weight gain.

OTC products that people use for sleep are often filled with other medications that we don't need. Nyquil for instance works well, but it contains multiple unneeded medications, unless you are sick. The most used sleep aid is Tylenol PM, which is simply Tylenol mixed with Benadryl, but unnecessary Tylenol can be bad for the liver.

Sleeping medications work for a while, but then our bodies start building up a tolerance to them. Some sleeping medicines are quite addictive as well. People with insomnia would be safer if they see their doctor rather than buy over-the-counter sleep aids.

There are good prescription sleep medications today that work quickly, improve the sleep architecture, and don't have any morning "hangover."

Many clients who happen to require a sleeping medication say they "bounce" out of bed in the mornings when they use any of the non-addicting sleeping medications that we frequently prescribe at the Day Program in Dallas: Sonata, Ambien, or Lunesta.

Genetic perfectionism—usually a low serotonin problem, resulting in counting things, songs that won't leave your head, rechecking things too many times, hoarding, self-critical messages, compulsive rituals of any kind, like hand washing or pulling out your own hair, and insomnia from worrying about what people think about you and about every detail of life (i.e., fear of making a mistake, etc.). Serotonin meds, like Cymbalta, Effexor-XR, Lexapro, Zoloft, or Prozac, will almost always eliminate these obsessive-compulsive traits.

Genetic dopamine "blue genes." If you inherit a dopamine imbalance, you can go one direction and develop Parkinson's or go a different direction and develop paranoia, which leads to insomnia. You may also feel like people don't like you or are out to get you, thinking your room is bugged or that you are being videotaped, or that demons are under your bed. You could even hear voices that are not really there or even see things—scary things—in your room that you would swear are real but are actually just a dopamine imbalance playing tricks on you. These delusions and hallucinations nearly always clear up within a week or two on the new and powerful atypical antipsychotic medications, such as Abilify, Geodon, Seroquel, Risperdal, or (if a person is anorexic and needs to gain twenty pounds) Zyprexa.

Genetic thyroid hormone "blue genes." Lots of people inherit abnormal-ities in their thyroid gland, which influences the brain and all other organs of the body. If the thyroid hormones are too low, you can have insomnia even though you feel very tired all the time, have dry skin, hair loss, weight gain, depression, serotonin depletion, and even psychosis (loss of touch with reality). If the thyroid hormones are too high, you can get manic and psychotic. Recently I admitted a suicidal college student with severe insomnia into our Day Program. As I got to know him, I found out he was a fine, loving Christian young man from a nice family. He usually behaved quite normally. At that time, though, he felt demons in various parts of his body and was delusional and couldn't sleep. I couldn't find any significant psychological or spiritual reasons for his psychotic depression, and he had no family history of it. But he did have a family history of thyroid abnormalities, so I ran a series of thyroid tests on him and he had almost no thyroid hormones in his blood. I gave him thyroid hormones daily and some serotonin and dopamine medicines, and he cleared up quite rapidly, back to his normal behavior. But I warned him to have his thyroid followed by a medical expert in that field to keep his levels normal.

A wide variety of genetic illnesses induce insomnia. Your body and your brain heal more at night than any other time, so a good night's sleep is vital. Don't be ashamed to take nonaddicting sleeping medications if you need them. Sleeping pills like Ambien and Sonata are not physiologically addicting, even though anything (including candy) can be psychologically habit forming. They are also safe, unlike some of the "natural" sleeping aids, like melatonin, St. John's wort, or SAM-e, all of which are dangerous if combined with various medications.

Another aid to sleep is proper nutrition. See chapter 10 for more details about nutrients and vitamins and how they relate to your thoughts, feelings, and general health.

GOOD NIGHT, SWEET DREAMS

Here are some practical tips for good sleep and sweet dreams when insomnia is not due to "blue genes."

Develop a close personal relationship with the real God. Get to know the God of the Bible, who died on a cross for you and stripped to His undergarments to wash the feet of His friends. Would your earthly father do those things? If not, then ask God to show you who He really is, and have daily and nightly friendly chats with Him. Even tell Him when you are angry with Him. He knows everything anyway, so you might as well discuss it with Him. There are lots of horrible things that happen to us and to others that we will never understand until we get to heaven, so have a little trust that He knows what He is doing by giving depraved humans so much free will.

Get enough sleep so that you wake up most mornings naturally before your alarm clock rings. If you sleep too little, it will deplete your serotonin, which builds up at night while you are sleeping, and you will become less efficient and more depressed. If you like to have early morning devotions, try to go to bed early enough to wake up refreshed, before the alarm clock rings. If you can't form this habit, schedule a different time for daily devotions.

Use the hour before you go to sleep in a positive, relaxing way. Don't do your physical exercise right before you go to bed. Also, don't argue at night in bed.

Get rid of grudges daily. Don't go to bed angry. In fact, try to resolve any anger situation at least an hour before you go to sleep. The Apostle Paul taught us in Ephesians 4:26-27 that we can get angry at people without sinning, but it becomes sinful when we go to bed with the anger stuffed and unresolved. So resolve it before bedtime, then unwind in a positive way before going to sleep. Satan loves grudges and bitterness because he knows he can use them to deplete your serotonin and render you less useful to God. Ask God if you are holding grudges toward anyone who may have hurt you in the past. Forgive that person and turn vengeance over to God, remembering what He promised in Psalm 68 and Romans 12.

Some people sleep better if they have a warm bath before bedtime to relax them. Others rest better if they take a mildly cool shower, then go to sleep in a cool room, especially a quiet room with no noise and preferably darkness, or perhaps a small night light. A comfortable mattress is a must (since you spend one-third of your life in bed!).

In order to sleep well and have good dreams you have to have serotonin in ample supply floating in the synapses (spaces) between your billions of brain cells. You cannot eat serotonin. If you did, it would not digest and go into your brain. You cannot take serotonin in medicine form for the same reasons. So your options are to eat a small snack with tryptophan in it. Bananas, milk, dairy products, and meats, especially turkey meat, are high in tryptophan. It's not a good idea, though, to eat protein before you go to sleep, because it takes a long time to digest. A little milk would be fine, but in order for tryptophan to cross the blood brain barrier, the tryptophan has to have Vitamin B6, and a few carbohydrates with it. If you're on the Atkins diet, it's better to modify it with small amounts of carbohydrates with your tryptophan.

Whether you turn to medication, nutrition, or new behaviors, we trust the ideas and insights in this chapter will help you and yours find the way to true rest. Our desire is that you might love and be loved, have good days and nights, a meaningful life and sweet dreams based on the scientific, psychological and spiritual insights you gain from this chapter and the others in *Blue Genes*.

Chapter Four

Baby Blue Genes

Jane was a wife and mother and full-time missionary in Brazil. She loved God, her husband and her two children.

Though Jane had experienced some degree of postpartum depression after the birth of her first two babies, she recovered without medication. But following the birth of her third baby, she got so depressed that she became psychotic and planned to kill her husband, her three children and herself. If she had carried out the plan, she would have been totally innocent, because she had no idea what she was doing.

God intervened in a miraculous way before Jane went through with her plan. The head of her mission group in Brazil called to ask me what to do to protect the lives of Jane's family members and to cure this young mother who was now ready to kill, or kill herself, or both.

I named an antipsychotic medicine that I knew they would have in Brazil and told her to get Jane on this medicine immediately and make sure she took it daily. Missionaries would have to fly with Jane to the U.S. for me to treat her, and they would have to stay awake in shifts while Jane slept to be sure she wouldn't kill anyone.

She was immediately admitted to our Day Program in the Dallas area, where our team worked with her every day. I started her on a better antipsychotic medicine (the best ones at this time are Geodon, Abilify, Risperdal, and Seroquel). Her husband bravely stayed with her in the hotel room, even though his life was in some danger. Another friend stayed so they could sleep in shifts, never leaving Jane unattended.

Within three weeks, she was herself again, though weeping over the fact that she nearly killed her family. She has been fine ever since that episode. In addition to medicating her correctly, we allowed her to express her ambivalent feelings and deal with her own childhood issues.

James 5:16 says that if we confess our faults one to another, and pray for each other, we will be healed. Therapists see this verse come true daily. Jane will probably stay on the antidepressant and antipsychotic meds for a year or so, then she and her husband and I will all decide together whether to drop her two medications, one at a time, and risk having her illness return.

If her stress level is better than it was in Brazil, she will probably do fine off the meds. But if she gets any bizarre thoughts, she will restart the antipsychotic medicine immediately to keep her from doing something she has no idea she is doing, like a robot with a short circuit.

—PAUL MEIER, M.D.

Why is it that about 80 percent of women have some degree of post-partum blues, especially after the first baby? In reality, this high percentage should not be especially surprising.

Little girls grow up playing with dolls—usually dolls that they hand pick, or are given by Mom or Grandma. They get to play when they want, and when they are tired, they conveniently put the dolls to bed, even if it's only ten in the morning. Many girls have special dolls that wet when squeezed, or cry when turned upside down.

Little girls also read and watch fairy tales where the frog turns into a prince and sweeps the princess off her feet before both get to live happily ever after. But real life seldom turns out the way we idealized it in elementary school. In real life, a girl grows up, gets married to "Prince Charming," gets pregnant, and starts her pregnancy by vomiting every day for the first few months.

Then she (and sometimes the "Prince") go to birthing classes where they tell her that if she does the right exercises and is truly brave and spiritual, she will certainly have a natural childbirth without any of those epidurals or other "non-natural" chemicals. Moreover, if she does it right, it won't even hurt (even though the Bible promises in Genesis that "in pain you will deliver your babies").

Most pregnant women are excited to be part of the miraculous process of producing a human being, but they are also afraid of the awesome responsibilities, such as being tied down and coping with increased financial pressures.

Some fear they will make so many mistakes that their children will grow up to hate or humiliate them. In a well-intentioned attempt to be a "perfect Christian mother," a woman might feel guilty about these normal ambivalent feelings that all women have. So those feelings get buried and ignored.

These feelings may show up in dreams. For example, the mother gets in a car wreck and lives but the baby dies. This doesn't mean the mom really wants the baby to die; it simply means she has normal ambivalent feelings and is afraid to become aware of them. If these ambivalent feelings are severe enough, they can lead to panic attacks.

It is healthier to talk about your ambivalent feelings about having a baby openly with nonjudgmental friends or relatives, because James 5:16 promises that sharing the truth about any flaws you see in yourself brings about healing. We see this verse working every day in our psychiatric practices—spiritually, emotionally and physically.

A shared burden is only half a burden. Confession relieves much of your ambivalent anxiety immediately as you share it and own up to your faults and struggles without inducing any self-condemnation. Romans chapter 8, verse 1 reminds us that there is *no* condemnation for believers.

The Bible says that Satan is our accuser, so legalistic Christians who might condemn you for having normal ambivalent feelings may be unconsciously working for him.

Some women feel "ugly" when they are pregnant; however, the two most beautiful word-pictures that God ever created to show His love to humans are a woman carrying a baby and a woman breast-feeding a baby with nurturing milk from her own body. One of the names God chose for Himself to show us what He is like is El Shaddai, which can be interpreted, "God of the breast." He is the God who loves us and wants to nurture us with Himself.

Finally, delivery day arrives, and a woman tries to do all the right breathing, but it still hurts worse than any pain she has ever experienced. She might feel falsely guilty if she had been told delivery would not hurt if she only did it right.

Then the labor lasts eighteen hours instead of the two or three she anticipated. "Prince Charming" arrives a little late because he was on the last hole on the golf course and had to finish his game.

The doctor arrives and says he will need to make a cut to let the baby out (an episiotomy), so he strongly recommends some anesthesia. The delivery results in a blood loss, which leaves the mother anemic. This means she is more likely to become tired, more depressed and more irritable.

Iron deficiency leads to even more fatigue and depression. Of course, the baby doesn't wake up and sleep when it is convenient for mom. He wakes up and cries when she is exhausted and he sleeps when it's time to show him off to Grandpa or another guest. To make matters worse, when Mom looks in the mirror, she still appears to be in early pregnancy, which is a big disappointment to her.

Prince Charming doesn't really wake up in the middle of the night to change the diapers like he said he would. And Prince Charming's mother moves in for two weeks to help out, rearranging all the furniture and giving unwanted advice.

When you were little, your baby doll only wet when you squeezed it, cried when you turned it upside down, and woke when you were bored and had nothing better to do. But a real baby wets all over you, and has earwax coming out his ears, belly-button crud, a runny nose, dirty diaper, and basically something gooey coming out of every hole in his body.

What anemic, "hormonally challenged," tired woman with all this pain and stress, in her right mind, would not get at least somewhat depressed? Let's worry a little more about the 20 percent who don't experience any depression after the birth of a baby than the 80 percent who do. They can apply for jobs as movie actresses in "Stepford Wives II."

This is not even taking into consideration that five percent of all women and men inherit a high degree of perfectionism, which makes postpartum depression more likely since perfectionists have a lower serotonin level to begin with, plus they want everything to run perfectly, which never happens.

They are already stressed by changes, even the happy change of having their first child. In addition, 50 percent of all women and men have a higher than average predisposition to getting a serotonin depletion under stress; so having a baby, especially a first baby, creates a great deal of stress in most cases, resulting in postpartum blues or at least "postpartum blahs" in 80 percent of women, whether they have a genetic predisposition to depression or not.

Sally Monk was a wonderful young lady, a wonderful wife, a great friend, loyal to her siblings and parents, active in a healthy local church, and a great accountant. Sally got pregnant for the first time after five years of marriage, at age thirty-three. Her husband Calvin was supportive of her and excited about her pregnancy, even though it was not really planned.

They decided mutually that she would quit her job when the baby came, and they would scale down their lifestyle and expenses somewhat. The company Sally worked for loved her and her work so much that they told her she could work part time out of the home, which she accepted.

Being somewhat perfectionistic had given Sally a lot of benefits in her life. She earned excellent grades throughout her school years. She received a scholarship to college and also toward her M.B.A. She lived a very moral life except for some mild rebellion in college. She was a disciplined Christian, with daily devotions, prayer and the other spiritual disciplines.

But being a perfectionist can also be a handicap in some ways. Perfectionists like to help others, but hate to ask for help for themselves. Perfectionists like to feel in control, so when they are sick, they often hate to run to the doctor (although some go to the other extreme and become hypochondriacs, running to the doctor worried that every little symptom is a major catastrophe). They usually hate to take medication, although they may spend a hundred or two hundred dollars a month on all sorts of health food products that may be totally worthless.

When Sally got pregnant, she reluctantly saw an obstetrician and took the prenatal vitamins. She enrolled in classes that taught her that with the right exercises, she could have a relatively painless, natural childbirth. She was so into natural things that she insisted on having the baby delivered at a midwife location not affiliated with any hospital, so her obstetrician fired her as a patient after thorough warnings of the possible dangers to herself and the baby.

"Nonsense," Sally told him. "Women have been delivering babies this way for thousands of years."

"That's true," Dr. Feinstein answered. "But the death rate for childbirth has gone down for the mothers and the babies dramatically since women started coming to doctors and hospitals just in case an emergency arises." Sally assumed Dr. Feinstein was simply prejudiced and that she was certainly more knowledgeable than he was about what was right for her baby—another fault that gets perfectionists into trouble.

On the day Sally went into labor, she had everything totally in control. Her mother was scheduled to stay with her for a couple of weeks. Sally had even mapped out a rigid schedule for her baby to help her child turn out "disciplined" like she was. She did not make her house child-proof, because she was determined to follow the baby around when it was old enough to crawl and slap his hand whenever he reached for a "no-no" so he would learn at an early age who was boss.

When Sally went into labor, she beeped her husband and he met her with great joy at the birthing house. The labor lasted eighteen hours and Sally sucked up the pain as long as she could, but she had intense labor pains in spite of all her correct breathing and her husband's help.

The baby was a little larger than anticipated and could not quite move through her birth canal. The midwife did not have the necessary equipment or training to handle this emergency and was too over confident to have a backup physician and hospital arrangement. The baby girl and mother both almost died, then the baby finally managed to get out, but not without brain damage that she would have to live with the rest of her life on earth.

Then Sally's milk wouldn't come until the third day of breast-feeding. This, of course, caused more threats to the baby girl, little Jennifer, and to the mother's sanity, as she became extremely anxious at all the major disappointments. She carried guilt and shame for thinking she knew more than she did, and felt rage toward the people who misled her. Her own mother, who delivered Sally 33 years earlier at her own home without even using a midwife, was just one of many targets for her rage.

The baby was much more difficult to raise than Sally could ever have imagined. Little Jennifer did not adapt at all to the rigid schedule that Sally had been taught was God's way to raise a child. Even though there is not a single Bible verse on when to feed a baby, whether or not to child-proof a home, and most of the other things she was taught by other perfectionists who thought they spoke on God's behalf, Sally chose to believe the perfectionistic opinions of others.

Sally became increasingly depressed and even suicidal. She could not have any knives in her kitchen because they caused her to have panic attacks. She was afraid she might use one on herself or the baby. But she refused psychiatric help because her legalistic church told her she should just depend on the Lord and prayer.

She stayed in this state of wishing she were dead for two years, following her mentally handicapped daughter around, spanking her hand many times a day, all day long, as the curious little girl kept reaching for expensive knick-knacks Sally had lying all around the house on coffee tables and such. By age three, not only was little Jennifer mentally handicapped because her mom refused to birth her in or near a hospital, but Jennifer had also developed obsessive compulsive disorder and was a very depressed child.

Jennifer had to eat the same foods at the same meals at the same times every day, lining up all her food in rows before she would eat it, or else she went into a panic. She had to have a certain glass, sitting in a certain space near her plate. She would only play with a few toys that had to always be in a certain order.

Jennifer violently attacked any other three-year-old who dared touch one of her toys or even moved anything in her house out of its proper place. Part of Jennifer's obsessive compulsiveness was inherited (a "blue genes" phenomenon), because Sally had done most of the same things when she was a young girl. In fact, Sally continued to count and recheck things over and over again even as an adult.

Sally hoarded magazines and newspapers and really just about everything, thinking she might want to read it or use it some time in the future. Sally hated to part with anything. Jennifer was the same way, hoarding whatever she could get her hands on without getting them slapped and hiding her food in strange places when Mom wasn't looking.

Jennifer probably would have turned out to be obsessive compulsive even without any "blue genes" pointing her in that direction, simply because of the rigid way she was raised. If parents refuse to childproof their home and punish the crawling infant for doing what God intended her to do—explore and learn—then that child becomes more perfectionistic.

She also becomes more of a rigid thinker, afraid to have creative ideas because most creative ideas as an infant resulted in pain from getting her hand slapped. There is a time to spank a young child, but only for open, willful disobedience and defiance, and never severely enough to cause bruising. A child should never be spanked for healthy, God-driven exploration, or for making mistakes.

If parents remove all the "no-no's" from the infant's home and encourage exploration, that child will be more likely to be both left- and right-brained, more creative, more abstract in her thinking, and less likely to be brainwashed as an adult by some cult leader. She will also be less likely to marry someone who is rigid and controlling.

The continually hand-slapped child may be a good mathematician or good at a job that just requires repetition. But that child is unlikely to become a good scientist or artist.

Sally's husband, Calvin, an associate pastor of a large church in the Chicago area, became tired of being around a chronically depressed, picky, critical, obsessive compulsive wife and a beautiful but mentally handicapped, depressed, obsessive compulsive three-year-old daughter. He confided regularly in a woman whom he had been counseling for a year as her pastor. Those sessions ended up with her counseling him and expressing pity for his situation, as well as awe at how amazing he was. Calvin came to the conclusion that God had predestined him to marry this counselee, Raquel, but that Calvin had been out of God's will accidentally when he chose to marry Sally.

One Thursday afternoon, when Calvin was "counseling" Raquel a little after normal hours, while the church was otherwise empty, the janitor walked in on Calvin and Raquel having an intimate moment right there in Calvin's recliner. The janitor turned Calvin in to the head pastor, in spite of pleas and even offers of large sums of money by Calvin and Raquel.

Calvin lost his job. Raquel divorced her husband, and Calvin divorced Sally, married Raquel and moved to another state.

In the meantime, Sally eventually fell in love, over a long period of dating, with a very kind, "hang-loose" and loving man, John, who per-suaded her to come to the Meier Clinic Day Program for treatment of her obsessive-compulsive disorder and chronic depression. Sally was still reluctant to do this, and the thought of confessing all her secrets to a group of strangers was quite frightening to her.

She probably would have always been too proud to do such a thing, but she really loved John and felt greatly loved by him. Deep down she knew it would probably help prepare her for marriage and for life with at least a little more insight and knowledge. She did not really believe we could get her over her depression.

In fact, she spiritualized her depression, thinking it was a good thing to have, so she could suffer with Jesus and with the pains of humanity. But within a few days of seeing the deep love and compassion and outpour-ing of tears and God at work in the lives of the other patients, Sally changed dramatically herself.

She always was a basically loving person, hiding behind the walls she had built up as a child as a result of rigid parenting by her mom and dad. She also inherited a genetic tendency to have a low serotonin level, a "blue genes" problem that contributed significantly to both her depression and her perfectionism.

The counseling took care of the root problems, allowed her to grieve her losses, got her in touch with her feelings, and even taught her how to ask others for a hug, for advice and for love. By taking Cymbalta (an anti-depressant medicine that builds up serotonin and norepinephrine), she was freed from her depression and obsessive-compulsive habits within seven weeks. The Day Program counseling gave her tools to connect on a gut level with people and to stay emotionally healthy.

Sally left the Day Program after three weeks, feeling significantly on the road to recovery. She and John went for pre-marital counseling and eventually got married. They ended up having three more children and a very happy life. I still see her for a fifteen-minute medication check once every three months, and she has been very happy and faithful to God and to John for four years now since they got married.

GETTING HELP POSTPARTUM

Life is tough enough for the 80 percent of people with no severe mental biochemical deficiencies. But the more "genetically challenged" your family tree is, the more likely it is that you may need some temporary psychiatric help (especially during the postpartum period). Possibly even some anti-depressant medications would help as well. You're at a definite advantage if you breast-feed your baby because prolactin acts as a natural antidepressant and antipsychotic agent.

So for those of you who are normal human beings and *do* experience some degree of postpartum blues or at least postpartum blahs, consider the following suggestions to lessen your pain.

Realize that with the loss of blood and possible anemia, the loss of sleep, the hormone shifts, and all the changes in your daily routine that are forced on you (out of your control), it is normal to have some degree of postpartum sadness and even a little healthy self-pity.

Some Christians think self-pity is a sin (and wallowing in it forever probably is), but if you feel pity for your best friend when she is going through a stressful time, is that a sin, or is that being like Jesus? Of course, it is what Jesus would do: "He pities His children." Well, you are just as important to God as your best friend is, and I urge everyone to become his or her own best friend, so a little self-pity is a godly thing to practice, not a sin like Satan and his assistants would like you to believe.

Remember that Jesus said in the beatitudes that He would bless those who become sad and cry, and that He will personally comfort them. He loves you intensely. You are one of His best friends. He created you in your own mother's womb so He could enjoy you forever.

Go ahead and cry whenever you feel like it, without being embarrassed.

If you don't let your anger and sadness out, they will deplete serotonin in your brain and lead to a more severe clinical depression. Remember again, "Blessed are they who mourn…."

Find an understanding friend who will empathize with you and listen to your ambivalent feelings without condemning you or laying a guilt trip on you. You may need to find someone other than a family member.

Family members want to help, but they often say things like, "You should just be thankful to God you have a healthy baby, when so many other babies have birth defects." Statements like this just worsen your false guilt. Remember, it was Jesus who told us to weep with those who weep, and that there is no condemnation to those who belong to Him (Romans 8:1).

BREAST-FEED IF YOU CAN, AND DON'T FEEL GUILTY IF YOU CAN'T

Remember that when you breast-feed, your body produces prolactin to make the milk come to your breasts and release it to your baby. That prolactin is almost identical to some of the psychiatric medications psychiatrists give to patients who are depressed, anxious or even psychotic. That is why some of my psychiatric medications make women start to lactate even if they never had a baby.

Accept the changes in your body. If you got praised too much for your good looks growing up, you may base your self-esteem on your good looks now. That is always a big mistake for anyone, male or female. It should be based on your quality of character—your ability to love and be loved. But don't condemn yourself for wanting to get back in shape. If it is okay to mow your lawn or paint your house, it is probably okay to work on your own outward appearance a little.

Some women have genetic relatives who have schizophrenia, or who are bipolar, or who have experienced recurrent depressions, or alcoholism, or obsessive compulsive disorder (counting things, rechecking things, compulsive hand washing, hoarding, etc.). You may not have any of these inherited diseases yourself, but you are more likely to develop some degree of postpartum depression if you have this kind of genetic predisposition. So if you get just mildly depressed, then express your feelings, get some exercise, and try to get some sleep whenever you have an opportunity. Be sure to take some good vitamins, ask for help and an occasional babysitter, and you will probably feel better. But if your depression results in wishes that God would let you die, or if you have suicidal or homicidal thoughts, see a psychiatrist or your Ob-Gyn and get a good antidepressant. If the antidepressant blocks your ability to enjoy sex with your husband (usually six weeks or so after the baby is born), then either switch to a different one or add Wellbutrin-XL to your current antidepressant and the problem will usually go away. Your doctor may want to add a low dose of an atypical antipsychotic if you start developing a blank stare or keep losing your thoughts or develop any bizarre thinking or think you hear voices when no one is there. In fact, you should see a psychiatrist if this occurs to be sure you don't slip into a psychosis. Having relatives who have been psychotic means that it would be easier for you to slip into a psychosis than someone without any genetic history of it in their family tree. One out of every 33 people in the United States becomes psychotic (believing grandiose or paranoid delusions and/or hearing voices) some time in their lives, and postpartum is a vulnerable time for this.

In about three percent of postpartum depressions, the brain chemicals get so unbalanced, either due to too much stress or a genetic predisposition, that the woman becomes psychotic—more paranoid and even delusional. She may think strangers are talking about her, friends hate her, or that God will not save her. She may accuse her honest husband of having an affair. She may hear voices, but nobody is there, so she assumes they are demons or else God. The voices are almost always very critical of her. They are *not* demons (even though demons do exist) because they nearly always go away when a psychiatrist puts her on a medicine to correct her temporary dopamine imbalance.

If this describes you, get psychiatric help immediately, because you could end up harming yourself or a loved one. Really nice people do things like this when their brain chemicals are extremely unbalanced. Just recently, a postpartum mother a few miles from where I live went psychotic and cut off the limbs of her baby, killing the child. She had no idea what she was doing.

This is called a postpartum psychotic depressive reaction. It is purely a chemical reaction, and taking a dopamine medicine clears it up within a very short period of time. People who develop postpartum psychotic depressive reaction will become normal again, and may or may not need meds in six months to a year after recovery.

For those of you who are recovering from postpartum depression or even "postpartum blahs," it is important to remember that the recovery is gradual and uneven. You may feel a lot better several days in a row, then have one bad day and overreact and think, "All is lost. I am hopelessly depressed and will never recover. I might as well commit suicide."

You would be surprised how often this is heard in psychiatric practices. Be assured that postpartum depression is nearly 100-percent curable, either with counseling or with medications or both. Remember that Satan is the accuser of the brethren, and he would love to destroy you and make you believe negative lies. Be patient. God warns us about this in 1 Peter 5:8-9—to watch out for the Devil who is looking for victims to devour.

Remember the promise in 1 Peter 5:10 that "the God of all grace, who called you to his eternal glory in Christ, after you have suffered a little while, will himself restore you and make you strong, firm and steadfast."

Chapter Five

Paranoid Blue Genes

Ted, the pastor of a community church on the West Coast, was one of the nicest guys you could ever meet. He was a great dad to his kids, very kind to his wife (to whom he had been unhappily married for about 30 years), and an outstanding pastor in every possible way.

I met Ted and Hillary for the first time in my Dallas office. They were both so depressed that they checked into our Day Program for intense therapy.

Hillary was not grossly psychotic. In other words, she didn't hear any voices that others didn't. She didn't think people were following her, bugging her phone, poisoning her food, or reading her mind from a satellite. I did pick up on a distinct paranoia, and when I politely pointed this out, it elicited a sharp, angry reaction.

She was somewhat hostile, controlling, sensitive to constructive criticism, self-righteous, and condescending. Her attitude was critical toward Ted and pretty much everyone else around her. She hoarded books, newspapers, and magazines in their home, planning to read them someday.

Hillary happened to be the church secretary and tended to control Ted's life both at work and home. Ted's personality was passive and compliant. He privately confessed to me how he would give anything to break free from Hillary. However, he stayed in the marriage because he didn't have biblical grounds for a divorce.

We performed extensive psychological testing on both of them and interviewed two of their children. We also talked to a married couple that they had been friends with for over twenty years.

In the vast majority of cases I have seen, the husband and wife have an equal number of problems. But in this case, Hillary had the biggest problem, her paranoia, and flatly refused to acknowledge it. Hillary also refused medications, though she spent two hundred dollars a month on "natural" health remedies that were of no help.

—Paul Meier, M.D.

Where Paranoia Begins

It is important to understand that there are several ways people can become paranoid like Hillary. Sin is one way. When God lists the seven sins He hates the most (Proverbs 6), sexual sins are not even in the top seven. Number one on God's list of sins is a "proud look"—a look of arrogance, condescension, or self-righteousness ("I am right and you are wrong, and that's all there is to it!").

So pride is a sin that leads to increased paranoia. But bitterness (holding long-term grudges) is probably the greatest spiritual cause of increased paranoia. The more repressed anger a person holds inside, especially if not even aware of the anger, the more paranoid that person becomes.

Say that a psychopath bought a loving and cuddly puppy today, and for two years kicked the dog across the room each day before feeding him. Then a nice person, like you, approaches the dog for the first time. Do you think the dog would run up to you and lick your hand? The dog would almost certainly be paranoid from the years of abuse and would think you were probably as dangerous as his master. He would likely growl at you and might even bite if you came near him.

If you bought the dog from that mean man and treated the dog kindly from then on, petting him regularly and so on, the dog might eventually become friendly. He would eventually learn that not all humans are like his first master.

In group therapy at our Day Program, some people realize it was their parents who were sick. As children they learned to believe they were the cause of family conflict or even abuse. They grow up thinking something is wrong with them; they are not as good as other kids. This results in low self-esteem. We retrain their whole warped way of thinking. Our patients learn to like themselves. Without this new insight, many of them would continue carrying the parental verbal abuse toward themselves in their private self-talk, hating themselves for not being good enough.

Paranoid people lie to themselves often through the defense mechanism called "projection." If you put your hand on an overhead projector, it will appear as though your hand is on the screen, when in reality it is only on the projector. People who are paranoid and self-righteous deny their own faults. These people become uncomfortable hanging around with anyone (including their own children) who may have a similar fault, even if the fault of the other person is trifling.

The Bible describes this defense mechanism in Matthew 7:3-5. Jesus addresses our inclination to see the toothpick in someone else's eye while ignoring the log in one's own eye—a sign of hypocrisy and paranoia.

Pride can lead to paranoia, which leads to a spirit of being untrusting and holding grudges against people, often for minor incidents. Paranoid people think others are out to get them or at least intend to mislead them. They begin to falsely predict others' behavior, much like the puppy expected every human to be a psychopath.

HILLARY'S ROAD TO RECOVERY

A thorough life history of Hillary revealed nice parents with no history of any type of abuse. She recalled no history of bitterness or large disappointments in her life. She did admit that she had always been untrusting and suspicious of other peoples' motives. She also remembers that shadows and noises scared her more than they did other kids. Thoughts that a monster might attack her continually terrified her, especially at night.

Hillary's paternal grandfather had paranoid schizophrenia, which is a disorder that includes paranoia, delusions (false beliefs), and hallucinations (hearing imaginary voices and seeing imaginary objects). Several cousins on her mother's side of the family also had schizophrenia.

When Ted married Hillary thirty years earlier she was beautiful, a strong leader, and a committed Christian. He did notice she was a little legalistic, like the Pharisees were in Jesus' day, but he overlooked it. A few months into marriage he began to realize that whatever he did was never good enough to please her.

Whenever there was a disagreement, Hillary never conceded that she was wrong; it was always Ted. She also never apologized for anything. As time went on she became more controlling and emotionally "cold." This couple, quite affectionate while dating, never kissed or even held hands anymore.

Ted's mother had also been somewhat paranoid and controlling, so he was used to that type of behavior. Since history usually repeats itself, about 85 percent of people marry someone similar to the parent of the opposite sex. This is usually fueled by an unconscious dynamic.

We performed some psychological testing on Hillary, which showed she most likely had mild schizophrenia. The good news is that this condition is very treatable.

One of the first rules in psychiatry is that you can't force someone to talk before he or she is ready, nor can you tell the client too much about his or her personality before gaining trust. If you do, it will push the person away; often you will never see him or her as a patient again. Choosing the right time to approach Hillary with this information was critical.

After a few weeks in the Day Program, our team had begun to win some trust from Hillary. In our weekly treatment team, where all the doctors, nurses, and therapists discuss the progress of each patient, we decided it was time to tell Hillary our conclusions.

We shared the results of her testing as well as a family diagram we had drawn showing how her paranoia could have been passed down genetically from both sides of her family. I explained this was a neuro-chemical imbalance of dopamine in certain parts of the brain and that we could correct it.

She didn't believe us, of course, but had built up enough trust that she continued in the Day Program. The next day I reasoned with her that if I was wrong and she did not have a chemical imbalance, then taking a dopamine correcting medicine every day would not change her behavior. She did agree to try the medication for one week, but this was only to prove that I was wrong and she was right.

She swallowed the medication in our presence each morning to show that she was really taking it. I've learned from past experience that para-noid patients will often only pretend to take medications or do what we call "cheeking" and spit the pill back out when no one is looking. We actually have pills that melt in your mouth now that prevent this.

By the next day she was quite a bit sweeter, and within three or four days she was a different person. She was friendly, but with appro-priate assertiveness. She also shared appropriate anger instead of "leaking" anger any time she felt like it.

Ted fell back in love with his wife, this time with her real person-ality. I say "real" because it was her real personality without the dopamine imbalance. The paranoid Hillary was not at all the "real" Hillary, but Hillary with a chemically defective brain—much like a defective computer or a car without the right kind of gasoline.

—PAUL MEIER, M.D.

If a person has paranoid "blue genes," he or she will exhibit the paranoid traits listed above throughout much of life. Although schizophrenics may be quite normal early in life, they usually begin to exhibit more paranoia and decreased social interest when they are in their teens or twenties.

They often start isolating from other people, may dress eccentrically, and have weird beliefs and interests. This often culminates in a "psychotic break" where the person starts hearing "demon voices" and loses touch with reality.

Even though the onset seems sudden when a psychotic break happens, it usually isn't and there has been a gradual, many times unnoticed decline. Family members of schizophrenics will often, after the fact, recall several years of increasing paranoid and eccentric behavior before that first psychotic break. In fact, psychiatrists can now look at the old home movies of a family where one child developed schizophrenia, and without knowing anything more about the family, three-fourths of the time these psychiatrists can pick out which kid will be the one to develop schizophrenia. Even youngsters often show subtle behavior differences from other children.

If you have this illness in your genes, then why don't you have schizophrenia at birth? Scientists believe these genes are not "turned on" until the teens or twenties. Many of our genes do not become active until a certain point in life. For instance, you are born male or female, but the genes that develop you into a man or woman do not turn on until puberty. That point can be a different age for each person. Also, it is a gradual process. You don't change from a boy into a man in one day.

Blue genes are the same way and can be dormant for years and then become active. Some people's blue genes never become active, but sadly most do.

Christians sometimes wonder how we know the voices that schizophrenics hear aren't actually demon voices. After decades of treating hundreds of patients claiming they hear audible demon voices, we have seen these voices disappear on the right doses of the right medication 100 percent of the time. So either the voices are caused by the chemical imbalance, or else most "demons" are allergic to psychiatric medication and flee the body of the victim.

We do believe in God, angels, and demons and what the Bible says about them. Demons work in subtle ways to deceive and cause false guilt, making believers inefficient for the cause of Christ. Jesus called them the accusers of the brethren. This method of influencing Christians is more common than that of speaking in audible voices.

Schizophrenia is a devastating disease that affects one percent of the population. However, many people, like Hillary, inherit a mild dopamine imbalance and are paranoid in their personality features without being grossly delusional or hearing audible voices.

People can also see and hear things without being schizophrenic. Severe depression and bipolar can both cause paranoid delusional behavior. Drug use can definitely lead to delusions and paranoia. Some medical illnesses, like hyperthyroidism (overactive thyroid gland) and Alzheimer's disease, can have these same symptoms. These symptoms are still caused by an imbalance of dopamine.

Symptoms Preceding a Psychotic Break

Before someone experiences a psychotic break, there are five possible symptoms. Notice that each begins with the letter "A."

1. Affective Disorder. Patients largely lose the ability to laugh or cry and develop a "flat affect," which is often manifested by a blank stare. Psychiatrists use "affect" to describe the range of emotion they observe in a person. A hysterical person who goes quickly back and forth from laughing to crying has a "wide" or "labile affect." If someone you have known for a long time suddenly develops a blank stare and their eyes seem larger and spacey, and they become more like a robot instead of a laughing, crying, feeling human being, this person probably has a dopamine imbalance. The best medications we have for this today are Abilify, Geodon, Risperdal, Zyprexa, and Seroquel. They are known as atypical antipsychotics. The pharmaceutical companies are now calling them "psychotropics" since doctors are using them for much more than psychosis. The older antipsychotic or neuroleptic medications, like Thorazine, Haldol, and Navane, work well on psychosis, but still leave the patient with a very flat affect. They also have many dangerous side effects if taken for a long time. State hospitals and prisons still use the older ones, mainly because they are less expensive.

2. Associative Disorder or loose associations. These people can't hold a string of thoughts together. Sometimes the person will lose his train of thought in the middle of a conversation. This is called "thought blocking." It happens to all of us once in a while, but much more often when dopamine is out of balance. The person may even make sentences that seem to make sense to him but don't make any sense to you. His thoughts and speech often wander from subject to subject (called "tangential thinking").

3. Anhedonia—the loss of pleasure. Hedonism is the Greek word for pleasure and "a" is a prefix meaning none. It is the inability to have fun and laugh with your friends. Anhedonia is one of the main symptoms of depression.

4. Ambivalence. This is the coexistence of two imposing impulses toward the same thing in the same person at the same time. Here's an example that will make more sense: When someone calls a friend or family member and threatens to commit suicide, he is ambivalent. On one hand, he feels like he wants to kill himself, but on the other hand, he doesn't and is crying out for someone to help him not feel that way. Ambivalence in psychotic people describes how, on one hand, they show no emotion (laughing or crying) at all, but may become violently angry for no reason. This violent anger may lead to that person killing himself or someone else. Ten percent of schizophrenics kill themselves, but 50 percent will at least attempt suicide. One-third of all homeless people in the United States are schizophrenics who could live a relatively normal life if they would take medication. The problem is not the treatment, but rather because they refuse it as many paranoid people do. There are schizo-phrenic patients who are successful pastors, business executives, teachers, and so forth. Other patients might do well for fifteen straight years, then they convince themselves they're cured and don't need medications. Their symptoms usually return again within a few weeks. This often happens after the first psychotic break. That person refuses to believe they have any condition that needs continued treatment.

5. *Autism.* This is not childhood autism. Rather, autism in schizo-phrenia is the process of becoming more and more withdrawn from the real world. This is sometimes the first sign of a dopamine-related mental illness. These patients may seem in a daze and may not even answer when you call their names.

WHAT ABOUT "RELIGIOUS DELUSIONS"?

We have worked with literally hundreds of psychotic individuals over the past thirty years, and our experience is that Christians have "Christian delusions," Muslims have "Muslim delusions," Buddhists have "Buddhist delusions," and atheists have secular or more political delusions.

Christians who become psychotic often become delusionally grandiose, thinking that they possess supernatural revelations or abilities. Many think they are God Himself.

In one instance, three people out of eight in group therapy all thought they were Jesus. One was even a woman. They argued with each other over which one was Jesus. These were intelligent, responsible people who had become psychotically depressed. One was a pilot for the largest pas-senger airline firm in the world. It is fortunate that he lost touch with reality while on the ground rather than while flying 500 passengers to Europe, because he might have heard God the Father's "voice" telling him he was Jesus and should fly the plane home to Heaven.

When I did his physical exam upon admission to the Meier Psychiatry Unit of the hospital, he refused to give me his urine sample after he had filled up his cup. When I asked him why he wouldn't give it to me, he said it was because it was now "holy water."

I invited my pastor to come and persuade my airline pilot patient to give up his delusion that he was Jesus, just using Scripture and prayer. I had not started the pilot on antipsychotic meds yet, since he had just been admitted, so this was a window of opportunity.

The pilot had become a Christian as a ten-year-old, and had studied his Bible all his life since then. He had been a very committed Christian, active in his local church, until his psychotic break.

After two hours of examining all the predictions about Jesus in the Bible, and proving to this pilot that if the Bible is true, the pilot could not possibly be Jesus, the pilot scratched his head a moment, then turned to my pastor and calmly said, "And to think all these years I thought the Bible was true."

The pilot gave up his belief in the Bible, but continued to be convinced he was Jesus—until we gave him antipsychotic meds that corrected his brain's dopamine imbalance. Within a few days, the pilot was back to normal, believed the Bible again, and was embarrassed about what had happened to him.

I assured him it was not his fault. It was a biochemical imbalance caused by some stressful situations and his blue genes predisposition.

—PAUL MEIER, M.D.

Unfortunately, many Christians around the world who become delusional and grandiose have enough charisma to gain the trust of naive individuals. Look at the writings of the founders of many cults for evidence of that.

In general, as the dopamine imbalance worsens, the more grandiose and/or paranoid the person becomes. In these delusional states the person often feels wiser and more powerful than anyone else. In addition to the neurochemical abnormalities, this could also serve as a defensive reaction to severe inferiority feelings.

The more inferior a person feels, the more grandiose he tends to fool himself into thinking he is. People who hate themselves, possibly because of abusive childhoods or chemical imbalances, usually find scapegoats to whom they can transfer their self-hatred.

Many families have disowned each other because of paranoia, projection, and scapegoating. This is defined as displacement. Your hostility is placed onto an innocent victim rather than the actual person you are hostile to. Real-life examples of this are when someone is mad at his boss but takes it out on his family. The hostility is usually transferred to a victim who is less threatening or more defenseless. In many families this person is one of the children. The oldest child often suffers more hostility or rejection from the same sex parent.

The authors hope that by the end of this book, you will understand all sorts of "blue genes" that family members can inherit, or similar problems we can develop from sin, abuse, or even physical brain trauma. There are depressive "blue genes," bipolar "blue genes," ADHD "blue genes," perfectionistic or even OCD "blue genes," sociopathic "blue genes," shy "blue genes," even paranoid (dopamine imbalanced) "blue genes," as we have explored in this chapter.

The good news is that medical knowledge is doubling every five years now, in large part due to the computer age. Many "blue gene" factors affecting behavior, thinking, and emotions can be improved or corrected with modern medicine.

Chapter Six

Loneliness Blue Genes

James Teale was a 42-year old man. Extremely shy and depressed, he considered suicide on a daily basis. His parents recalled he had been shy even as a small child, though his siblings were quite extroverted. He had a maternal uncle and a paternal grandmother with social phobia, however.

James managed good grades in school, but he wasn't interested in sports or other extracurricular activities. He had a few friends, but never any more than one close friend at a time. James had very little interest in church and rarely attended church youth group functions or school parties.

In college James became even more isolated. He did meet one young lady, Whitney, who actually pursued him for dates. He married Whitney in his junior year of college, but the proposal came from her, not from him.

Their relationship lacked intimacy, but that didn't seem to bother Whitney because her family was, as she described it, "emotionally detached." James and Whitney had two children soon after the marriage, Caleb and Joy.

Despite James' shy, withdrawn personality he became a successful

*businessman, owning a large furniture store. During the day he dele-
gated most of the responsibilities to his employees while he retreated to
his office in the back of the store, rarely meeting or mixing with
employees.*

*At night, James went home and had dinner with his wife and
children. Both kids were socially well adjusted, in spite of a very limited relationship with their dad. James would often bring a novel to
the dinner table and read it while the other three carried on a normal
conversation.*

*James was a very nice man who tried to be a good father. He was
kind to the children. He would listen to them if they shared their problems with him, but he showed very little emotion and seldom offered
advice. When Whitney or the children would hug James and say, "I
love you" to him, he would stiffen slightly, then give them a token hug
and whisper, "Me too."*

*James professed to be a Christian, though he rarely went to church
or attended any religious services. Every time he had to be among
people, he felt an uncomfortable nervousness almost to the point of
nausea. His main fear was making a fool out of himself in front of
others. He did read his Bible from time to time, and he did pray privately, but he seldom discussed his religious beliefs, even with his wife.*

*On the outside it appeared James had it made—with a lucrative
business, attractive wife, and nice children. On the inside he was a
complete mess. The lonelier he grew, the more he contemplated suicide.
Sensing that he might actually carry out his suicide plan, his wife and
sister convinced him to fly to Dallas to attend the Meier Clinic Day
Program there.*

*Once there he admitted that suicide seemed much easier than par-
ticipating in therapy groups with other people. He had never opened up
and interacted honestly in sharing his true feelings with anybody. He
was there mainly to satisfy his wife and had no expectations of
improvement.*

The counseling staff asked about a hundred questions regarding James' symptoms, family life, spiritual attitudes, and much more. At last he was diagnosed with social phobia, an anxiety disorder in which people avoid crowds or attention because of intense anxiety.

Though his case was more extreme than most, James is not alone in his isolation. Loneliness is epidemic in our culture. Children, teens, and adults of all ages are lonelier now than ever in the history of mankind. There is more human suffering caused by loneliness in this generation than any generation since Adam and Eve saw one of their sons murder the other. This seems paradoxical since there are now more people on earth than ever before and we have the luxury of more available free time than any other generation.

In this chapter we will discover how genetic biochemical imbalances can lead to loneliness. We'll also talk about loneliness as it results from poor choices or reactions of self-protection we have habituated into our behavior patterns. When people you have trusted emotionally injure you, one instinct is to close down, thus preventing further injury. We then become fearful of intimacy and learn to live in an ongoing state of loneliness, a painful condition that can eventually progress to suicide.

A comprehensive survey of ninety thousand teenagers (published in *The Journal of the American Medical Association,* September, 1997) revealed that one percent had lost a parent to suicide in the previous twelve months. Over seven percent of the teens surveyed had, themselves, made a personal suicide attempt in the previous twelve months.

These teenagers reported having many superficial friends and acquaintances, but revealed they also felt lonely and isolated from intimacy. The teen suicide rate, abortion rate, drug and alcohol abuse rate, and other similar negative behaviors had increased by 75 percent in the last ten years. Based on earlier, less extensive studies, these factors had increased by 300 percent compared to fifty years earlier.

So what changes have been made in our society in the past fifty to sixty years that have driven us to this greater degree of loneliness and despair than ever before in the history of mankind? The AMA which is somewhat liberal to begin with, had to at least allude to the fact that a higher divorce rate, a lack of value-based education, and the replacement of intimacy with sex and drugs were major factors in the decline of our society. The journal even surmised that homosexual teens were much more likely to be lonely, abuse illegal substances, and commit suicide. The happiest and best adjusted teens were the ones fortunate enough to live under the same roof with both parents. These teens also reported spiritual connections in church youth groups and a strong group of close, accepting friends.

In the past fifty years, misled groups like the Civil Liberties Union have promoted abortion, homosexuality, and the removal of all religious and moral education out of public schools. Today these groups even file lawsuits to keep the Ten Commandments from all public buildings. They pass out condoms to teens, encouraging "safe sex" rather than abstinence until marriage.

These groups have eroded the commitment levels in marriage today. They sanction an easy "no-fault" divorce and taxation by our government of couples who marry (thus penalizing the institution of marriage), while giving tax breaks to couples living together without marriage. Couples who live together before marriage, by the way, have a seventy percent higher divorce rate than those who don't.

The factors just mentioned are among the reasons why loneliness is at an all-time high. At all the Meier Clinics across the country, we see teenagers and young adults every day. In our initial evaluation we usually ask about a hundred questions trying to hone in on the correct diagnosis.

This type of evaluation also helps us determine how much of their pain is coming from "blue genes" and how much from early childhood development. Sometimes their problems are simply caused by poor choices they have made. Others have had a life filled with trauma.

Our goal in therapy is not to blame parents, as many people think. Our goal is to speak the truth in love, even if that does mean looking parental abuse squarely in the eye. We work hard to bring about family restoration whenever that is possible.

Have you heard the joke about the golfer who decided to get golfing lessons from a psychiatrist? After several lessons the golfer's friend asked him if his golf score had improved any. The golfer replied, "No, but at least now I know it is all my parents' fault and not mine!"

That's not what true psychiatric help entails. A good counselor looks at everything an individual has learned from his parents and significant others in his life—separating the true from the false by comparing the information to what the Bible says about those subjects. The goal is to help the person stop operating on false beliefs, such as: "Since my parents hurt me when I was three years old and I tried to get intimate with them, I'll fear getting intimate with people the rest of my life." When this happens, it often results in a painfully lonely person who replaces intimacy in life with sex, drugs, alcohol, "workaholism," or even "churchaholism."

Yes, it is possible to become a churchaholic. That is someone who goes to numerous church services each week and serves on so many church committees that he or she can avoid emotional intimacy through busyness, superficial meetings, superficial fellowship, and "do good" projects. God definitely desires for us to serve Him in some capacity, but this service should not replace emotional intimacy with our families.

Many psychiatric problems also lead to loneliness and isolation. People with depression, paranoia, and anxiety socially withdraw from others. Those with ADHD and bipolar mania tend to push others away.

ADHD teenagers report more loneliness than other teens. This is largely due to some social awkwardness that accompanies the disease. They unknowingly turn others off with dominating, interrupting, and impulsive behavior. However, with social skills training, and medication if needed, these teens do well with others. With proper treatment of any psychiatric condition, loneliness will decrease. Lonely people are rarely happy people and vice versa.

Most of you reading this book can probably think of a family in which all the children are well adjusted emotionally except for one. This one child is usually very introverted, uninvolved in any school clubs or groups, and spends most of his free time alone. Even though he attends school, he remains isolated as much as possible from the other kids.

Solitary occupations such as computer work, accounting, or engineering attract these people, because of the limited interactions with other people. These people may remain single throughout life, though they sometimes marry. The marriages are often rigid and cold with little intimacy. Many times these people marry someone like themselves.

Even though this is the life they have chosen, these people often end up chronically depressed. They are also at high risk for addictions. Remember, it is impossible to be happy in life without some degree of loving others and being loved by others. But loners fear intimacy because their faults might be exposed. Often addictions become a substitute for intimacy. For example, pornography can appear to substitute for intimacy with a real person, because it gives the user a sense of power without having to be vulnerable.

The problem with addictions, though, is the enjoyment is usually only for a season. Sadly, thousands of lonely people like the ones described above commit suicide every year. How many of these people were lonely? How many of these people were depressed? How many of these people's lives could have been saved by treating their depression or befriending them in their loneliness? Many, I suspect.

Suicides outnumber homicides in the United States by almost two to one. Suicides tend to run in families as well. Does that mean there is a "suicide gene"? Probably not. A gene does not make you grab a gun and shoot yourself. But there are "blue genes" that lead to psychiatric problems that do lead to suicide. Eighty-five percent of those who commit suicide have an underlying mental illness.

Think about your own family. If there have been suicides, be aware, and don't be afraid to ask for help if you need it.

SOME KEY QUESTIONS

With this information on how loneliness can be influenced by genetics, environment, and life choices, I want you to ask yourself three simple questions.

1. How loving am I to myself? Do you say negative, derogatory things to yourself that you wouldn't say to Jesus or to your best friend? If you do this, expect to be lonely. You haven't even decided to love yourself yet. You can only love others as much as you love yourself in a biblically correct way. Jesus said, "Love your neighbor as yourself." How can you love your neighbor if you don't love yourself?

Put today's date inside your Bible cover, and write the following statement: "I, _____, promise myself from this day forward to be my own best friend. In doing so, I will change my self-talk. I will not say anything to myself that I would not say to one of my best friends. When I get furious with myself for making mistakes, I will replace my fury by saying, 'Welcome to the human race. All humans make mistakes. I would rather be a person who makes mistakes but can love and be loved just as I am.'"

Now sign and date this promise to yourself.

2. How many friends do I have who know all of my secrets and love me anyway, unconditionally, in spite of all my faults? The Book of James says we all fail in many ways, so quit expecting yourself to be perfect—you can't! Choose one or two people of the same sex, and/or your mate. If you consider these to be "safe" people, start being more honest about your needs, wants, and emotions. If they reject you, it's their loss. It proves that whomever you chose wasn't the kind of person you wanted to get close to anyway. The Bible tells us that if we want friends, we must show ourselves to be friendly. In other words, friends don't grow on trees; you have to develop them over a period of years. Many people want friends, yet take no steps to make any. You can't just sit home and expect people to come knocking at your door asking to be friends.

Be careful not to trust someone until that person has earned your trust over a period of time. You can choose to give a person love, but you should wait to give a person trust. Love is free and unconditional. Trust is earned and conditional, and that's the way it is supposed to be.

The middle verse in the Bible (Psalm 146:3) says not to put your trust in man. But remember that the Bible also says that our love and intimacy level is what shows the world that we are disciples of Jesus.

If you are too shy to ask someone to be your friend, then join a Bible study group, Celebrate Recovery Group, bridge club, or a gourmet club—any group that meets weekly and is made up of safe, godly people. Over a period of time, you will find your personality attracted to one or two other members of that group and become intimate friends in this more indirect manner.

3. Do I chat with my Heavenly Father; His Son, Jesus; or the Holy Spirit every day? Do you spend time every day in silence, listening for God to tell you something? Do you look for what He may be telling you in your dreams? There are over 150 passages of Scripture on dreams alone, including Psalm 16, where we are told that God speaks to us "even at night."

Eighty to 90 percent of the patients we see in our practices say they don't have a single friend who knows all their secrets. These are very successful people—business owners, physicians, pastors, homemakers, engineers, teachers, and political leaders from various countries, etc.—from all walks of life.

James 5 says that if we confess our faults one to another, and pray for each other, we will be healed. All kinds of healing can result from confessing our faults, failures, and feelings to significant others who will continue loving us in spite of these things.

The group therapy sessions in the Meier Clinic Day Program practice James 5:16 several hours a day. Patients share the sad and happy experiences of their childhoods. Some have heart-wrenching stories that include all kinds of abuse.

All young children want to love their parents and be loved in return. It is very sad to hear how some people never experienced this. For many people these negative experiences affect their personality greatly today.

Some leading psychologists say that 85 percent of a person's personality is formed by the sixth birthday. But Philippians 4:13 says we can change our personality, with God's help, no matter how old we are. If our moms and dads encouraged us to be honest about our feelings (even if angry), listened to our feelings, valued our feelings, and gave us affirmation, then we find it quite easy to love and be loved as adults. But if they ignored us, we will believe the lie that we aren't worthy of being noticed. We get "don't exist" messages from them, even nonverbally, and then wonder why we can't love others or allow others to love us.

If we were punished for being honest about our anger and other emotions, we learned to become intellectual and suppress our feelings. This leads to repressing emotions as a way to protect ourselves from the rejection and loneliness we felt as young children when we were aware of our feelings and shared them openly and honestly.

If our parents were verbally, physically, or sexually abusive, the lies we came to believe about ourselves are even worse:

- I'm trash.
- I deserve to be abused.
- I'm so bad, my good parents had to abuse me in disgust.
- I'm disgusting.
- No one who knows all my innermost thoughts and secrets would possibly love me.

• God doesn't even love me. How could He?
• God may not even exist, or if He does, He seems off at a distance. (Remember that most people who do believe in God think He is like their fathers or mothers.)

These are the kinds of lies we hear every day from very intelligent and financially successful patients, who are also very lonely. Even in their loneliness they continue to push people away and avoid intimacy, even intimacy with God.

They still fear getting hurt, as they have been in the past. They figure loneliness is better than the hurt of rejection. If they do make an honest attempt to love and be loved by someone, it is a very slow process to knock down all the walls of protection.

I absolutely love an old song that was sung by Paul Simon. In fact, I still listen to it on a regular basis. The name of the song is "Something So Right."

In this very psychologically and philosophically deep song, Paul Simon sings about the Wall of China, a thousand miles long. He says that to keep the foreigners out, they built it strong.

But Paul confesses that there is a wall inside of him that nobody can see. It is an invisible wall of protection from emotional intimacy. Paul sings, "It took a little time to get next to me!"

Paul implies in that song that because of past hurts, he expects rejection, loneliness and pain. He expects things to go wrong. And when things do go wrong, he tends to take the blame whether he is part of the cause or not.

But now he is falling in love with a wonderful woman who makes him feel so right that he feels confused. He is not used to loving and being loved intimately, and it feels so right and good that he thinks something must be wrong because he never felt something so right before.

What a beautiful song, and so deep. God created us to love and be

loved. He wants us to find safe people to connect to now. Psalm 68 says
God takes the lonely and places then into new families. So get fathered,
mothered, "brothered" and "sistered" now!

—PAUL MEIER, M.D.

You may wonder, "How is it I can send a hundred Christmas cards to friends and relatives yet still feel all alone in the world?"

It happens all the time, and Paul Simon's song explains a lot of it: as two- and three-year-olds, we have all made attempts to love, to be loved, to weep and grieve, to empathize, to help someone else, to protect our property from being taken or destroyed by another kid, to laugh, to share, and even to start figuring out who God is.

We were probably all more in touch with our true feelings at age two than we are now. When we were mad, we said so. When we were sad, we were not hesitant to cry. When we felt lonely, we looked for someone to fellowship with. We were amazingly in touch with our emotions.

But then something backfires. We express anger at a parent and get punished severely for it, which teaches us to deny our anger from then on. We push our feelings down and learn to live with our loneliness. Yet loneliness—which is probably the number one cause of emotional pain in this world—can be overcome. We can replace loneliness with genuine loving and being loved.

Loneliness is a prison. Many people do their own life sentence in this psychological prison. The most heartbreaking part is that the key to get out is always available. Yet there are a thousand reasons why some people never reach out for the key: "I don't believe in mental illness." "My church said my problem was lack of faith." "I want to treat this the natural way." "How can doctors help a spiritual problem?" "Talking about my problems will make them worse."

Knowing the root reasons for loneliness can provide a key to escape.

While loneliness is often caused by blue genes, it may also stem from the influences of environment and life choices. Marilyn's story, told by Dr. Paul Meier, provides a perfect example.

MARILYN'S STORY

Marilyn Tayliss was a 38-year-old famous and very beautiful movie star who constantly arrived at the hospital complaining of multiple physical problems. She always felt tired and weak. A team of physicians from several different specialties examined her and ran almost every lab test they knew of, but still found nothing.

They diagnosed her with somatization disorder, which usually means there is an unknown psychological problem resulting in physical symptoms. These people have frequent headaches, stomachaches, muscle aches, and other vague illness symptoms. They sometimes get diagnosed with "chronic fatigue syndrome" or "fibromyalgia."

When traditional medicine cannot find a physical abnormality, these people often turn to alternative types of medicine. They may spend thousands of dollars getting weird tests performed such as fingernail or hair follicle analysis. Many of these studies now claim to have the ability to measure brain chemical levels, which is actually not possible at the time of this writing.

Her doctors finally told her they thought her physical symptoms were caused by depression. She reluctantly agreed to see me for a psychiatric consult. Marilyn was dressed very seductively in a "see through" negligee at our first meeting in her hospital room.

She immediately began telling me how she was going through her eighth divorce. This last husband was an alcoholic who physically abused her, ran around on her, and even bragged about it. As we talked, it turned out that all of her husbands had been cheating, alcoholic abusers.

Marilyn spoke about her devotion as a Christian and was a little surprised when I asked her, "Don't nice, Christian guys ever ask you out when you are single? After all, you are attractive, easy to talk to, wealthy, and a 'movie star.'" Marilyn replied, "Yes, but they are so boring!" Here was a person with millions of adoring fans, millions of dollars in the bank, and eight ex-husbands, but she was one of the loneliest people I had ever met.

I usually ask patients about their childhood during the first interview. In this case I didn't need to. I had a strong suspicion as to what her childhood had been like from the way she avoided intimacy now. "Can I take a guess as to what your childhood was like?" I asked.

"Fire away," she replied with a smirk on her face.

"I would guess that your father was an alcoholic who ran around on your mom. He was open about this and probably beat your mom when she complained about his behavior," was my answer.

Her smirk turned very serious as she asked, "How did you know that?"

"Just a lucky guess," I replied. What was my first clue? It's estimated that up to 85 percent of us marry someone similar to the parent of the opposite sex. Many of us even do this unconsciously.

"Can I have one more guess about your childhood?" I asked.

"Sure," she replied.

"Your father sexually abused you at some point in your life, didn't he?" She was stunned and admitted, "Yes, from age thirteen to seventeen."

She then became furious, as she recalled how her mother never protected her. She accused me of speaking to her mother because she had never told a single soul about this except her mother. I told her I didn't need to talk to her mother to guess that someone who would marry eight men in a row who were addicts, abusers, and cheaters must have had a father like that also. It was an unconscious attempt to "fix" or "replace" her father.

At this point she asked me to get out of her room and never come back.

A day or two later she asked to speak with me again. This time she wanted help and agreed to try our Day Program. There, she gained insight into her root problems.

We used no medications—just Christian-based counseling to help overcome her codependency issues. She was able to get in touch with her true feelings, which led to weeping and grieving over her losses.

Think about this example, please. Every day each human makes at least some choices he believes he is choosing. In reality, his unconscious is working for him, just as in Marilyn's case, where she believed she was choosing eight wonderful husbands.

Interestingly, Marilyn's physical ailments such as migraines, chronic fatigue, sore muscles, and stomachaches all went away after counseling. She said this was the first time in her life that she ever felt happy and confident on her own and didn't feel like she had to be with a man. She has continued to do well. Up until this time she still remains unmarried, but I am confident that if she does ever take that step again, this time he will be a nice, loving, faithful, spiritual man.

TREATMENT FOR ANXIETY

For a person like James, introduced at the start of the chapter, assertiveness therapy and medications that help alleviate anxiety will improve social phobia symptoms. These people will never be as outgoing as the actor Robin Williams, but they can overcome much of their shyness, learning to interact comfortably with others. Relating to others is crucial in business, and social phobia could have definitely ruined James' career if it had remained untreated. He was close to fully normal within one week of taking Neurontin. His counseling took much longer, however.

Fear of speaking publicly (stage fright) is a symptom of social phobia but does not by itself constitute the disease. This can also be overcome with assertiveness training and/or medications. An estimated 50 percent of the population has a fear of public speaking. Interestingly, the number is much higher in adults than children.

Medicines that work on serotonin and also the GABA receptor help with social phobia. Severe social phobia can lead to a lonely, miserable life.

The newer atypical antipsychotic meds, which regulate dopamine, also help a great deal.

Even a blood pressure medicine, Atenolol, can help many overcome social phobia, but we do not recommend it except as a last resort, because some people get suicidally depressed on it. The other meds mentioned above all help people be not only more relaxed, but nearly always more happy as well.

When shyness or loneliness permeates almost every area of life it is known as avoidant personality disorder. People with this condition try to live a quiet life receiving as little attention as possible. Embarrassing situations often bring on panic attacks.

Antidepressants such as Zoloft, and Prozac are FDA approved for social phobia, but our experience with hundreds of patients gives us the impression that any modern serotonin medicine would probably make a big difference within ten weeks or so. A physician has to be very cautious when treating social phobia or any of the anxiety disorders.

If the dose of medication is started too high, it makes patients more anxious and can even precipitate panic attacks. This is called the "paradoxical effect," making something worse before it gets better. Doses have to begin very small, often one-half of the lowest strength pills. The dose is then gradually increased over the next few months.

GABA-enhancing medications like Neurontin, Gabitril, Depakote-ER, Keppra, and Topamax can be added for quicker anxiety relief, or can be used by themselves. They usually relieve nearly all of the social phobia symptoms within a couple of weeks. Lamictal also works well, but we don't understand all of its mechanisms yet.

When James Teale came for treatment, I tried Neurontin on him, climbing fairly quickly to 800 mg twice a day, and he was over his social phobia within five days. He still needed therapy to learn relational skills, assertiveness training, getting in touch with feelings, etc., but his phobias were gone in five days on Neurontin.

Some lonely people are so perfectionistic and afraid of medications that I have them take the pills home and just lick them once every night for a few nights. These people tend to have "side effects" on every medicine a doctor gives them.

They aren't faking it. They believe it. But what is almost always actually happening is that they are so afraid to trust an authority figure (like a doctor) that taking any medicine from a doctor makes them feel out of control. They can take 300 dollars a month of dangerous "natural" products from a health food store that they, themselves, pick out, but not even an aspirin from a doctor. They go into a panic when they try the medicine, so they have heart palpitations, hot or cold flashes, shakiness, dry mouth, choking sensations, diarrhea, nausea, etc.—all anxiety symptoms. But the patient is *sure* these symptoms are side effects of the medicine the doctor gives him.

I don't believe we physicians should ever be dishonest with a patient, but I will tell you about one exception I justified in my own mind. Sara Pitts was so shy and lonely and perfectionistic that she absolutely felt like she was going to die every time she tried any medications.

She was fifty years old, single, lived alone, and worked in a back room of a major corporation filing things. She had been extremely shy all her life, and had many family members with social phobia as well.

I really believed we could make her normal in a week or so on meds, and wanted to so badly, but I almost had to give up on her. Every possible medication to cure her "loneliness blue genes" brain chemical imbalance caused her to have what felt like a "near death" experience, even when she took only a tiny dose of medication for a few nights.

So, rather than give up, I did what I was taught to do 30 years ago, something that would be considered unethical now. I had the hospital pharmacist make up some capsules and just put a little sugar in the capsules. I knew Sara put lots of sugar in her coffee every meal, so I thought that would be the safest thing to put in the capsules. We made up a name and told her this was a new medicine that had no side effects.

I told her this was our last chance, so even if she had side effects, I wanted her to tough it out and keep taking the meds until her body got used to them and she stopped having side effects. She had the same violent side effects on the sugar pills as she did on the others, but she did tough it out, and the symptoms became less severe every day.

Finally, she had no side effects, but no real benefits either, of course. Then I told her what I had done, and that it was a last resort, and asked her to forgive me for deceiving her. She was angry at first, but then realized for the first time how her body created panic symptoms to meds, and that she really was NOT allergic to anything. Then she picked out one of the meds I knew would work, out of the list we had already tried. By letting her choose, she felt more in control than she would if I had picked. She had no side effects on it this time, and within a week she was over her social phobia, but still needed lots of counseling to learn intimacy skills.

—PAUL MEIER, M.D.

GABA medications are also excellent for reducing chronic pain, treating epilepsy, for general anxiety and leveling out mood swings. Another recent use, which at the current time of writing this book warrants more clinical trials, is in helping recovering drug addicts reduce cravings.

These medications also help curb alcohol cravings, which lowers the risk of relapse. Many shy people become alcoholics for several reasons. For one, the alcohol goes to the GABA receptors, so it temporarily "cures" shyness or social phobia or even a public speaking phobia.

Have you ever watched the talk shows, like David Letterman's or Jay Leno's, and noticed how many of the movie stars have to get drunk in order to come on the show for an interview? They may be very shy without alcohol or illegal drugs (like marijuana), and then dance on Letterman's desk in front of millions of people when "under the influence."

And since loneliness is probably the main cause of depression (along with repressed anger), "pot" or alcohol numb the pain for a little while at a time. When alcoholics who drink heavily stop drinking they run a risk of seizures or delirium tremens (DT's), which can be fatal. GABA medications help prevent withdrawal shakes, and seizures.

Drug addiction science is an exploding field, in large part due to the huge toll drug abuse exacts on our society. New research estimates that approximately 20 percent of Americans drink alcohol at levels that are harmful to their health. This excessive alcohol use interferes with the treatment of many other health conditions as well (e.g. hypertension, diabetes, gastroesophageal reflux disease, depression, insomnia, and gout). Europe, which is ahead of America in drug addiction treatment, is using GABA medications today rather than other addicting meds such as Librium, Ativan, and Xanax.

The Meier Clinics treat hundreds of people weekly for substance abuse and other additions, but detoxifying from heavy alcohol or drug abuse is so life-threatening that we always encourage those clients to go to Calvary Treatment Center in Phoenix, Arizona, for a month, then to come with a "dry brain" to our Day Program for another three weeks.

James, who had been shy all of his life, was just as outgoing as the rest of his siblings after a few weeks of treatment for his social phobia. This allowed him to mingle freely with his customers and employees for the first time and also grow more emotionally intimate with his wife and children. He was truly a new man. As he continued in the Day Program we worked on his social skills. He had been so shy before that he was still quite socially immature. We still see him three or four times a year as an outpatient in our clinic. He continues to do very well.

Fred Chambers was a single, 37-year-old truck driver who was not only shy all of his life, in contrast to his other siblings, but was also quite paranoid. Whenever he saw two or more strangers talking he assumed they were saying bad things about him. He heard negative voices that he assumed were demons, telling him he was "no good," or to kill himself, which he seriously considered many times. In fact, he drove his 18-

wheeler gasoline trucks in a manner that endangered his life and the lives of others on the road.

Fred was lonely and not only disconnected from intimacy with others but from reality itself. We treated Fred with Abilify, an atypical antipsychotic medication that works to restore balance of both serotonin and dopamine.

Within two weeks Fred no longer heard voices or felt others were talking about him. He also reported that for the first time he could remember in his entire life, he had not had any thoughts of killing himself.

Fred had been such a "loner" all of his life that he still needed about a month in our Day Program to help develop his social skills. Fred still has some eccentric ideas and behaviors, but for the most part he functions very normally. Since being discharged he has remained on his medication and in group counseling, and he reports enjoying every day of his life now for the very first time. Fred has paranoid schizophrenia, a very lonely life-long genetic disorder. But he is getting the best possible "wear" out of his genetic "blue genes."

You can too. We all can. Let's do!

Chapter Seven

The ADD Advantage

*Jack Tipton is a multimillionaire stockbroker and day trader. He has
enjoyed an adrenaline rush from taking risks all his life. He won
his neighborhood's boxcar race when he was six years old. His family
members were, like him, adventurers, so he was certainly not
overprotected.*

*Jack did high dives on the swim team, pole vault on the track
team, played catcher on the high school baseball team, and was a wide
receiver making dangerous catches on the high school football team.
Skydiving, scuba diving, motorcycling on trails, para-sailing, and snow
skiing on the black slopes were all norms for Jack.*

*His family was actually quite normal: loving, honest and hard-
working people. But they were all high-energy entrepreneurs and risk
takers and very successful financially. The difference between Jack and
the rest of his family is that Jack was definitely "wound the tightest" of
all of his family members. His highs were higher, and his lows were
lower. And Jack had trouble sleeping nearly 100 percent of the time.*

*During my initial interview, I asked Jack why he only slept four or
five hours a night. Jack replied, "Why would anyone want to be
unconscious when being alive and awake is so much fun?" I totally*

understood what Jack was saying, because I have had that thought my whole life.

But Jack had to be alert for his job, especially as a day trader, where he handled millions of dollars of other people's money in high risk trades for volatile markets such as corn, wheat, oil, gold, silver and even foreign currencies. The stress would be overwhelming for most people, but Jack was very smart and usually made good trades. He would wheel and deal on the phone, writing emails about totally different transactions at the very same time to other clients, and watching the moment by moment headline news scroll across the bottom of a TV screen on his desk. If he saw an international crisis suddenly pop up, he switched all his gears to be the first to invest millions of dollars of his clients' money in gold coins.

But the older Jack got, the more severe his insomnia became. He sometimes went a whole week straight without any sleep, unless he took huge doses of sleeping medications, and sometimes that didn't even work. Then he would dip into a major slump and be totally fatigued for several weeks, with the urge to withdraw from people.

During his energy surges with total insomnia, Jack began taking more risks than usual, losing large amounts of money for his clients and his company. During Jack's depressive slumps afterward, he became much more conservative than he had ever been, again losing his clients money they would have made if he stuck with his usual patterns of investment.

Jack had such a fantastic track record with his company for so many years that they did not fire him as they would have a younger man. But it came to a point where Jack was starting to become more irritable with employers and clients during his high-energy times, and his usual self-confidence became grandiose overconfidence.

So the owners of his company made Jack take a medical leave until he could get over this severe insomnia problem. They even paid his way to the top diagnostic hospital in the U.S. Jack checked into

that hospital where national experts ran brain scans, EEGs, blood tests,
and asked scores of questions to try to diagnose and treat his severe
insomnia problem. At the end of a three-week hospital stay, the lab tests
all came back normal.

They diagnosed Jack as having a "Sleep Phobia." This means that
they thought Jack's extreme fear of sleeping was keeping him awake,
and then the lack of sleep caused the serotonin depletion in his brain
that resulted in severe insomnia and major dips of depression and
withdrawal. They tried many different medications during Jack's three-
week hospitalization, but nothing gave him a single good night's sleep.
He wasn't any better off than before he went there.

So Jack's company flew him in their Lear jet down to Dallas, Texas
for another three-week stay at the Meier Day Program. Todd "Mark
Twain" Clements, M.D., and I did Jack's initial evaluation together. It
took us less than two hours to conclude that Jack simply had severe
ADHD and bipolar II. Just as Todd and the real Mark Twain are sec-
ond cousins, ADHD and bipolar II are also second cousins on the
genetic landscape.

—PAUL MEIER, M.D.

———

We knew Jack had ADHD from the results of the simple Meier Clinic
ADHD test, which is available for our readers at the end of this chapter.

We knew Jack had rapid cycling bipolar II because it is the only "blue
gene" disorder that causes a combination of severe insomnia with energy
bursts, racing thoughts, and hyper motor activity (they can't sit still very
long). They also usually have increased impulsivity, grandiosity, irritability, pressured speech, restless work (switching from project to project),
increased creativity (but not necessarily wise creativity), and poor judgment due to overconfidence not based on the reality of the situation.

The energy bursts occur generally every couple of months, last from
two to ten days usually, and then all of this is followed by a crash into

withdrawal, despair, depression, fatigue, and an increased risk of suicide. The depression often lasts a couple of weeks or longer, sometimes months.

Eighty percent of rapid cycling bipolar IIs, which is Jack's diagnosis, also have ADHD, and over 20 percent of people with ADHD have bipolar II (compared to less than 5 percent of the general population). People with ADHD and rapid cycling bipolar II nearly all have severe insomnia problems that are easily corrected with mood stabilizer medications.

The mood stabilizers are either GABA medications, such as Keppra, Gabitril, Depakote-ER, or else dopamine medications like Geodon, Abilify, Risperdal, Seroquel or Zyprexa.

In Jack's case, it was clear he would also need to have his severe ADHD addressed medically. This is usually best treated by the use of norepinephrine medications or dopamine medications (ruling out stimulants because they might keep Jack even more awake).

So we put Jack on a sedating GABA and a sedating dopamine medicine, just to play it safe, since Jack had not had a good night's sleep in years. We also improved his nutrition through vitamin supplements.

We also added Wellbutrin-XL (which helps the brain hang on to the norepinephrine and dopamine it makes), Strattera, a norepinephrine medicine and one of the best new adult ADHD medications (which is actually taken at night and helps people sleep at night and be highly motivated the next morning), and 200 mg of Provigil each morning (a non-addicting, histamine-related stimulant). In fact, our U.S. military pilots used Provigil during the Iraq War to stay awake and alert for twelve hours straight so they could drop the bombs in the right places.

Jack slept like a baby his very first night at a motel near our clinic. Within a week, Jack was feeling better than he ever had in his entire life. His wife and two daughters were with him and were totally shocked at how easily Jack was stabilized after years of trying different specialists and different medications.

Bipolar disorders are often treated with a single medication, but sometimes it takes a combination of five or six medications to help the brain work at its maximum capacity.

Jack not only slept great every night, he also had lots of energy every day. And his newfound ability to focus, relax, organize, and remember better not only helped Jack to do better than he ever had in his business, it also enabled Jack to invest more of his time and effort into things that are much more important than gold: his relationship to God, his wife, his daughters and to himself.

Dr. Clements has continued to see Jack once every three months for two years now, and Jack continues to love and be loved, sleep well, have sweet dreams and stay on his medications, knowing that without them, all of his symptoms would come back.

ABOUT ADHD AND THE ADD ADVANTAGE

ADHD can be a "blue gene" if it goes untreated and leads to low self-esteem and poor school performance. It can also be considered a blue gene if it decreases the potential of a human being who could have lived a normal life or often a better than normal life if properly treated. While ADHD and ADD are terms used interchangeably by the lay population, the technical difference is that ADD is ADHD without the hyperactivity.

Todd Clements is the Meier Clinic "expert" on ADHD, so he will describe its symptoms, causes and cures in the latter half of this chapter. Dr. Clements sees children, teens and adults for ADHD and all other psychiatric disorders. But Dr. Clements does not have an ADHD bone in his body. His focus and attention and energy levels are as steady as a rock, all the time. Two of the four authors of this book, however, David Mandt and Paul Meier do have rather significant ADD.

So we start this chapter on the positive side with a dialogue in which we share with you some personal stories about how we think we have an ADD advantage. Dave and I both firmly believe that we would not have accomplished nearly as much for God or mankind if we were satisfied with "mono-tasking" rather than living with the lifelong urge for "multi-tasking" that contributed greatly to our successes.

We both believe having ADD helped us to be too bored and impulsive to do regular jobs, and that God designed us as He said He did in Psalm 139, with unique strengths and weaknesses. ("You knit me together in my mother's womb. . . I am fearfully and wonderfully made.) For us, ADD gave us tendencies toward additional energy, multitasking, boredom and creativity, all of which helped both of us to take more risks and become founders of major organizations (The Meier Clinics and The Mandt System).

The ADD Advantage: A Dialogue Between Paul Meier and David Mandt

I (Paul Meier) have known David Mandt for about 26 years now. He is one of my closest friends. We have shared our most personal things with each other, prayed for each other, celebrated events together, wept together, and most of all, had a really good time hanging out together and being friends. I have great respect and admiration for David. Like myself, David has significant ADD. I help him find his keys all the time, and spell words, and he helps me whenever I get lost, which is quite often when I drive.

One thing I really admire about David is that he already had a great and successful life in his early thirties, with a wonderful wife and kids, a great church, and a lucrative job helping to run a multi-generational, family restaurant business. But when David felt God was tugging on his sleeve to pull him in a whole new direction filled with uncertainty, no guarantees, and the potential to lose everything financially, David, like Abraham thousands of years ago, took that journey of faith.

David took all his ADD traits, his devoted wife and kids, and left behind his financial security, listening to God for direction. At this point in his life he could have gone in quite a few different directions, because he is gifted in a number of ways, even though at times he felt ignorant because of his dyslexia and ADD.

He is quite an athlete, for example. I personally think he could have become a pro, but Dave denies this vehemently, even though he still hits 300-plus yard drives that are very accurate while in his early 60s. He was on the golf and gymnastics team in high school and junior college, and was a student pilot, scuba diver, water safety instructor for the city of Miami and later a Karate instructor. He was also a member of an elite Special Forces unit in the U.S. military (the Green Berets). He earned a Bachelor of Science in Radio-Television-Film at the age of forty-nine, earned a Master of Arts in Professional Development at the age of sixty-two, and has also done post-graduate work at Dallas Theological Seminary.

During those past thirty years since he left his security behind to follow the Lord's guidance, he has gone in a number of different directions, which a secular psychiatrist would think was all purely a result of the boredom and impulsivity of his extensive ADD.

But I know David Mandt and see God at work in David's and his wife Carol's lives and in the lives of their two wonderful adult sons. As his friend, and as a Christian psychiatrist who understands how God is continually leading us behind the scenes, I have seen God fine-tuning David. Being ADD, David and I both have handicaps to overcome. We both tend to think out loud. Unfortunately, that means we don't really know what we are going to say until after we have said it and listened to what we said, which gets us into trouble sometimes even with our mates and children.

I have done live national radio that has reached millions of people, often a million people in a day, for many years now. I have also been kicked off several Christian radio stations for openly sharing sins I committed that day or speaking my mind on controversial subjects without wording it carefully.

We both plead innocent and blame most of the trouble we get into in this regard on our genes. But in spite of his ADD and dyslexia, David has used all the training God has given over the years to develop him as an athlete, as an instructor, as a student of radio and TV presentation skills, and as someone who has learned from the loving confrontations of his wife and friends.

With this combination of things going for him, he has developed his own international business, helping thousands of people annually who have the potential to act out violently or to be violently mistreated. In fact in 2005, nearly all hospitals and other institutions that work with people who could potentially become violent have to undergo the kind of training that David's company, the Mandt System, offers in order to become accredited and receive insurance coverage. Dave's program is the best, in my opinion, and is nearly always listed in the top two or three by the accrediting agencies.

David risked everything financially in his early thirties in order to reach out and help protect people around the world using the Mandt System® (find out more at www.mandtsystem.com).

I believe God hand-picked David Mandt, who has ADD, dyslexia, and "foot in mouth disease" almost as bad as my own, to put a big dent in the violence so prevalent in the world today. His story should be a great encouragement to anyone with similar conditions.

PAUL: Dave, having introduced you, my first question is, how did ADD and dyslexia affect your life in your early years?

DAVID: Thinking back to my early days in school, I wish I had known that I had attention deficit disorder (ADD) and dyslexia (spelling problems). But back then hardly anybody knew it even existed and students with these genetic blue genes were simply labeled "dumb," "lazy," "undisciplined," and even "bad."

They were constantly punished for things they had no control over, and as a result, they developed low self-esteem. Many ended up with serious social behavioral problems, and some even ended up in prison. When good young boys and girls keep hearing that they are bad, they often become bad when they get tired of fighting against the label. This phenomenon is called a self-fulfilling prophecy.

I wish my parents and my teachers had known that I had dyslexia and ADD and that I was really trying to do the best I could. If I would have known, and they all would have known, I would have felt much better about myself. What a relief it was when I finally had that explained to me as an adult.

During those days (late 1940s through middle 1960s), I didn't fit the "mold" of the average student. I was easily distracted, bored, could not spell, had poor handwriting and had a difficult time learning to read, so I became a slow reader.

When my teachers or family members (who, of course, did not know I had ADD or dyslexia), became frustrated with me I would hear: "If you would just try, you could do it," "You just have to buckle down," "You're lazy" or the best one, "You're too smart to get such terrible grades." I would always ask myself, "If I'm that smart why don't I get good grades?" and my internal answer was, "I'm stupid." Those labels made a tremendously negative impact on my ability to perform in school when I was younger; but the ADD itself later became a blessing in disguise.

In middle school, I participated in as many school sports as I felt qualified to compete in and played soccer until I broke my leg. After middle school, I attended a military school, also a blessing in disguise because it had structure. As a person with ADD that is exactly what I needed. Military schools are well known for giving demerits, and early on, I received my share for not always meeting their standards.

If you received a certain quota of demerits, you weren't allowed to go home for the weekend or take part in other activities, and from this I learned to be responsible for my time and follow through with assignments. During the six years in military school my report card was sent home every week.

Although standard learning methods were a problem for me, I gained self-respect through other means, such as my military rank, drill team, athletics and friendships. I managed to keep learning, even though it wasn't through teaching styles that worked with the "average" student. I did very well in everything that was not academically related and somehow I made it through high school, which was the happiest time of my academic life.

Of course, my interests in learning were outside of "reading, writing, and arithmetic," and I picked up other information from a young age that influenced my future over time. I found out, for instance, that I learned best from watching and repeating what I'd seen. Excelling some in sports made up for my downfalls in the school system. I was on the track team one semester. I was the football trainer for four years, on the golf team for three years and was captain of the gymnastics team my senior year.

PAUL: What about after high school, David?

DAVID: My high school graduation gift from my parents was "permission" to take flying lessons. Learning to fly a plane wasn't like learning in school. I had to rely, instead, on common sense and learning by "hands-on" techniques.

As a student pilot with forty-plus hours, I was doing great. However, when it came time to take my written tests to receive my private pilot license, I never took the test because of my low academic self-image.

During the summer in my first years of junior college in Miami, I was a water safety instructor for the City of Miami and was an assistant Scuba instructor for one of the physical education courses offered by the junior college. All of a sudden, I was responsible for "teaching" instead of learning. As I taught children to swim, and students to scuba dive, I began to learn skills that made people feel good about themselves, and help keep them focused on what I was saying.

At the end of the two years at Miami-Dade Junior College, I went back to the family business. In November 1963, I joined the Army reserve. I guess in a way it was a chance to feel good about myself again since I had such fond memories of Riverside Military Academy.

PAUL: What was your military training, David, and do you think God used it many years later to help develop The Mandt System?

DAVID: In October 1963, at Fort Knox, Kentucky, because of my military training in high school, basic training for me was relatively easy because I knew one important fact. In basic training there are three ways to do things: the "right way," the "wrong way" and the "military way," and you had better do it the "military way." Because I knew that ahead of time, I was very successful. In fact, I earned the American Spirit Honor Medal, the highest award for a graduate in basic training.

After basic training, I was stationed at Camp Picket in Virginia for on-the-job training in radio communication, after which I returned to my reserve unit. I later transferred into an Army Special Forces reserve unit because they were doing a lot of interesting training and I wanted to be a part of that.

Again, since most of the learning was "watch, do and teach," I performed well in the system. While with the unit I attended and graduated from the Army Airborne Course for three weeks and was in contention for honor graduate, Parachute Packing Maintenance and Airdrop (Rigger) Courses for three months and was class leader, training at the Army's Mountain Training Course for two weeks, and in Special Forces Advanced Medical Training for almost a full year of training.

I thoroughly enjoyed the medical program. It was ironic, though, that I could perform minor surgeries, deliver babies, perform tooth extraction, and so on, but because I couldn't spell due to my dyslexia, I would never have survived traditional medical school. The military really improved many of my talents and skills and gave me a lot more confidence in myself and in my ability to help others by being part of a team. And, yes, Paul, I truly believe God used all of these things not only to help me to grow, but also to prepare me to help others.

PAUL: How did you feel, David, when you returned from the wide variety of military experiences to come back home to help run your family business?

DAVID: Each time I returned to the family business after the traditional seasonal break (a restaurant which closed during the winter months), I felt unchallenged and more dissatisfied with my work life. I was earning enough money during the mid 60s that my wife and I were making double house payments. We could buy almost anything we wanted, but it was difficult for me to deal daily with the boredom at work. My older brother was learning to run the business, and you can't have two presidents of a corporation, so there was no place for me to go. I felt as if God had something else in store for me.

PAUL: Now I can see how God used the ADD He allowed you to be born with to motivate you to have more variety in your life and not just maintain a monotonous job even though you were successful financially. I learned in my own high school economics class that everyone in life has to work his way up the occupational ladder, but it sure helps if your "old man" owns the ladder. Well, your dad owned the ladder, but you still left when you felt God leading you in a different direction, and I admire you for that. It was very courageous, especially after all the negative feedback you received all your younger years academically because of your ADD and dyslexia. So what was next?

DAVID: Since I felt insecure as a student, it was difficult to make the decision to go back to school. My earlier years in college were unproductive, and I played more than I worked.

With some encouragement from a neighbor, who happened to be a professor and head of the Special Education department at our local university, I decided to try a class or two to see if my age (early 30s) made a difference in my ability to learn. While taking these classes, I found tools that enabled me to make up for my learning differences.

For instance, I found that if I recorded the class lectures and typed out the notes, I had a better chance of retaining the information. I explained to my professors that it sometimes took me longer to read and comprehend test questions, and some of them gave me a longer period of time to complete exams.

PAUL: Did you have any idea that you would some day develop a system used around the world to de-escalate violence and protect not only patients but also the hospital staff who take care of those patients, as well as preventing violence in so many other settings?

DAVID: In 1975, while in the process of taking classes at the University of Texas in Austin and attending a local church, one of the psychologists at the Austin State School approached me with a problem. He said, "Dave, we need training for our staff that will reduce physical injuries between them and the people for whom they provide services. Could you come up with a set of standards that will help us?"

With my background as a water safety instructor, paramedic in the Special Forces, my background in gymnastics and body mechanics, psychology, etc., I somehow came up with some information that I thought would help. During the process, I kept in mind, "How would I want my family members treated if they didn't have the presence of mind to be in control of their behavior?" It was the Golden Rule: Do unto others as you would have them do unto you.

When I handed my friend the outline I developed, he said, "Would you come and teach this to our staff?" Thanks to word of mouth, I ended up not only teaching it to them, but also presenting my ideas at a six-state regional convention in 1977.

The program began to expand after that, and I found myself traveling and teaching more than working on my seminary degree. I was still sure that God had a purpose for me to fulfill, and I was sure it was through my original goal. Little did I know it was through the training He was allowing me to develop in managing behavior, which had now extended to developmental disabilities, mental health, public schools, hospitals, juvenile homes, foster care, child services, nursing homes, and so forth.

PAUL: Wow! It sounds to me like so many of the stories in the Bible. God seems to really like to use people that the world would not expect to be great successes, like little David, the shepherd boy, and Gideon, with no self-confidence, and Jonah, who ran away from God, and Rahab, the harlot, and Jacob, the deceiver, and so many others like them to accomplish some of His greatest works.

Maybe that is so God will get the credit, rather than man. In my own life, I was the poor son of a third-grade educated mom and a carpenter dad, but God gave me two dreams one night at age sixteen that took my own ADD world onto a different path. And God obviously did the same with you, David.

I think anyone reading this book will be encouraged by your life example to look not only at ADD and dyslexia, but at any other genetic "handicap" they or someone they love may have as something that God can turn around and use to His advantage.

We want all of our readers to realize that in our case, neither of us would have ever accomplished all we did to help so many people if it had not been for our ADD. For us, the ADD turned out to be an advantage that God used to enable us to do multiple tasks for Him. We would get too bored and impulsive to do otherwise. We had the ADD advantage.

LATEST RESEARCH FINDINGS ON ADHD

ADHD continues to become a more controversial diagnosis in America today. It is both the most underdiagnosed and overdiagnosed childhood disorder.

There are thousands of children who don't have genetic ADHD but are needlessly medicated on Ritalin, Adderall and other stimulants, just to make them "easier" to manage by parents and teachers. Some teenagers even fake the symptoms of ADHD in order to sell their stimulant medications to other teens.

Four to seven percent of children actually inherit attention deficit problems and/or hyperactivity and can function much better on proper medications. Many of these children are never diagnosed or parents refuse to allow them to receive treatment for the disorder. This is a shame because they often get labeled as "bad kids," "stupid," or "rebellious," when they are really suffering from an inability to concentrate and focus attention.

These kids report more loneliness, lower self-esteem, and more depression than children who don't have ADHD. Children with untreated ADHD have higher rates of school dropout, drug abuse, and legal troubles than kids who do receive treatment.

Medical researchers have shed much light onto the specific causes and treatments of ADHD in the last decade. We now know its transmission is highly genetic. It clearly runs in families. Studies of identical twins reared apart show that if one twin has ADHD there is a high probability the other twin will have it as well. Before that there were all sorts of theories as to what caused ADHD, such as bad diets, bad parenting, and brain injury. In the 1960s ADHD was called "minimal brain disorder."

The control of concentration and attention is a very complex process in the brain. It is actually controlled by more than one area of the brain, so if any one of these areas is not working quite right, it can throw off the whole system.

The frontal lobes in the brain, which control executive functioning, allow us to reason and also work to inhibit our impulses. This is why people with frontal lobe brain injuries are often very impulsive and explosive.

People with ADHD show decreased brain activity in the frontal lobes. In moderate to severe cases this activity decreases even further when they consciously try to concentrate. Dopamine and norepinephrine are the two brain chemicals involved in frontal lobe activity. Studies have shown how increasing the amount of these neurotransmitters improves activity in that area of the brain, which in turn means better ability to focus, calmer behavior, and less impulsiveness.

Stimulants like Ritalin, Adderall, and Dexedrine have been around for over 60 years. They work by causing the brain cells to quickly release more dopamine and norepinephrine. Regular Ritalin, for instance, works within minutes (an hour at most), but only lasts four hours.

When it does kick in, my ADD patients have a four-hour window of increased concentration and calmness. When it wears off they return back to their regular level of functioning. Fortunately, there are actually longer-acting forms of the stimulants out now that last all day. The medicine needs to be out of the system by bedtime so that the person taking it can sleep.

Stimulants are actually forms of amphetamine or "speed," as it is known on the street. One problem with them has been that while some people need them to function, others want to abuse them. Many kids are offered good money by "druggies" for their ADHD medicines. Wait a minute, how can taking speed actually slow you down? At low enough doses it helps improve the concentration, focus, and impulsivity of everybody.

Because of the abuse potential, doctors can only write prescriptions for a one-month's supply, with no refills. This means the patient has to come see the doctor every month, which is sometimes difficult for kids in school. The prescription cannot be phoned in to the pharmacy, and if the patients lose or have their medicine stolen, they're just out of luck until the end of that month.

Thankfully, we now have medicines that are not stimulants and are not abusable that help ADHD. Strattera has been on the market for a few years and increases the norepinephrine levels in the brain. We have seen good results with it in treating ADHD, more so in adults with ADHD than with children, but it works great for many children and adolescents as well.

Wellbutrin-XL is an antidepressant that also helps ADHD because it increases dopamine and norepinephrine in the brain. It is not a fast-acting releaser like stimulants, but builds up the levels over time. Ritalin works for ADHD within about five minutes of swallowing it.

Wellbutrin-XL takes ten *weeks* to reach a peak, so parents, ADHD kids and teachers have to all be patient with this one to see if it works or not. The advantage to Wellbutrin-XL is that the child, teen or adult who just takes it once a day, in the morning, and it works all day and night.

Ritalin helps a kid be normal at school, and then he goes home after it has worn off and drives his parents crazy with his impulsivity and forgetfulness and hyperactivity. On Wellbutrin-XL, the client is normal all day every day and doesn't drive anyone nuts. Another advantage to Wellbutrin-XL is that it makes smoking boring and tasteless, so parents don't need to worry about their kids picking up the bad habit of smoking if their kids are on Wellbutrin-XL, which is identical to the antismoking drug, Zyban.

Another advantage of Wellbutrin-XL is that it is an excellent antidepressant, and since suicide is the second leading cause of death in teens, having an ADHD medicine that also helps to prevent depression is a very nice safety precaution.

Wellbutrin-XL helps, after ten weeks, with energy, focus, concentration, memorization, and sexual enjoyment (but it doesn't make people want sex more). But for some people, it simply doesn't help ADHD as well as Strattera or Ritalin or Adderal.

With a married adult with ADHD, especially an older adult who may have mild difficulties with sexual enjoyment with his mate, adding this medicine can enhance the sexual quality of the marriage, which is actually very important to God according to Proverbs 5 and the Song of Solomon and many other places in the Bible.

The new antidepressant, Cymbalta, also shows some promise in improving ADHD. More time will be needed to know for sure how well it works. It has all the advantages of Wellbutrin-XL except it doesn't help people stop smoking like Wellbutrin-XL does. It is also approved for any kind of chronic pain or frequent headaches. So if an ADHD client has any kind of chronic pain problem, this could be the treatment of choice or else could be added to the stimulant medications.

Provigil is a new medication for narcolepsy that is also used to help our military pilots achieve better focus and concentration. It has a promising future in the treatment of ADHD as well, although it has not yet been approved for ADHD at the time of the printing of this book. It is not technically a stimulant and it is not addicting and it seldom has side effects.

Provigil is a great new discovery. You take it when you wake up in the morning, and it takes about an hour to kick in. Then you are wide awake for the next twelve hours and feel better in most cases, as it has some antidepressant qualities to it. You can focus and concentrate much better than normal when on it. If someone has ADHD and also is always tired and unmotivated, this would be a good addition. We don't know how or why it works so well yet, but it appears to be a simple histamine drug.

I have significant ADHD and have taken medications for years which increase my ability to concentrate and focus. For many years, I "toughed it out" without medication. But when I really thought and prayed about it, I decided that if I can take better care of my patients by having significantly improved focus and concentration, then it would probably be a sin for me to refuse meds.

There have been times that I went on vacation and, because of my ADHD, forgot to take my medications. When I come back to work my nurse, Lynne, usually asks me, "Dr. Meier, did you forget to take your ADHD medications on vacation?"

"Well, yes, as a matter of fact, I did forget. How could you tell?" I would answer.

Then she would say, "Oh, I can tell because you have been forgetting to put the dates on some of your prescriptions and making other little mistakes here and there that you normally don't make."

Another reason I gave in and decided to take meds for the past decade or so is because I want to have the greatest impact that I can for Christ. In my thirty-year career as a psychiatrist, I have written seventy

books; Blue Genes *is my seventy-first. The books have sold
millions of copies and have been translated into many languages
throughout the world, even Chinese and Korean.*

   *In the past decade, since I have been on ADHD meds, I have been
much more focused when I write, and much less distracted, unless my
favorite team, the Dallas Cowboys, is playing.*

                                            —PAUL MEIER, M.D.

TREATMENT FOR ADHD

When I (Dr. Meier) treat adult ADHD, I put them on liquid vitamins
(see chapter 10) because they contain phenylalanine, with vitamin B6,
which helps the phenylalanine cross the blood-brain barrier and produce
norepinephrine and dopamine in the brain, both of which may help
ADHD and help you see things more clearly and focus better and concentrate better.

   For more severe ADHD, prescription meds are needed, so I add
Provigil, especially for the pro athletes I treat for ADHD. It is not a stimulant but it works like one, enhancing their energy and focus for twelve
hours, eliminating their ADHD disadvantage and turning it into an
ADHD advantage. Sometimes I also add Wellbutrin-XL; it all depends
on various factors.

   Not everyone with ADHD needs medication. Particular diets do help
some people with ADHD, but usually a small percentage. Social skills
training is all that others need. Every child with ADHD, on medication
or not, should be involved in a social skills training group, as most
ADHD kids lag behind others in social maturity.

   About 50 percent of kids "grow out" of ADHD in late adolescence or
early adulthood. Another 50 percent continue to suffer with ADHD
symptoms well into adulthood, particularly inattentiveness and impulsivity. Researchers now believe that the greater the hyperactive component

of the ADHD is in childhood, the greater likelihood of symptoms continuing into adulthood.

In the next decade we will learn so much more about how ADHD works and cue in on safer and more effective treatments. We are considering it a "blue gene" in this book, and it definitely can wreak havoc in someone's life, especially if untreated.

However, there is another side of ADHD. It does have genetic advantages. When people with ADHD receive proper treatment we see these advantages flourish. Boredom and extra energy and impulsivity motivate lots of people to create new businesses and to diversify their daily routine. These things can result in great financial and creative successes.

A whole book could be written on the good aspects of ADHD and we hope to do that soon! We are just thankful that God is constantly helping scientists invent new treatments that help us live longer and more productive lives.

The following is a simple ADHD test, with only twenty "true/false" questions. The test will not only enable you to better understand the symptoms, but will allow you to see whether you or a loved one has ADHD tendencies genetically.

MEIER CLINICS BRIEF ADHD ASSESSMENT

Please answer the following questions as either "true"—meaning generally true, a fairly common practice, or "false"—meaning that particular practice or habit is one you rarely or never do. To be diagnosed as ADD or ADHD, the habits must be present before the age of seven. Some people do not inherit ADHD but develop ADHD-like symptoms temporarily during a stressful time in their lives. These symptoms will resolve when that stress is recognized and treated.

If you answer five or more of these first ten statements true (as a lifelong habit), then you probably inherited some degree of ADD.

_____ I sometimes forget appointments and obligations.

_____ I tend to misplace or lose things at home, school, or at work.

_____ I tend to be somewhat disorganized.

_____ I sometimes have difficulty paying attention to what people are saying to me because my mind is thinking about something else.

_____ I tend to make careless mistakes when I am doing a boring task or work assignment.

_____ I tend to lose attention when I am doing a boring task or work assignment.

_____ I tend to put off getting started on boring or difficult tasks.

_____ I tend to put off getting started on tasks that require organizing the task first.

_____ I tend to only partially complete tasks.

_____ I tend to daydream a lot and get easily distracted by noises or activities around me.

If you answer five or more of the following ten statements "true" (lifelong), you probably have inherited some degree of hyperactivity compared to the average person.

_____ I tend to interrupt others, even when they are busy.

_____ When my friends are talking to me too slowly or pause to search for words, I tend to finish their sentences for them.

_____ I tend to be more active than most of my friends, as though a motor inside me was pushing me to stay active.

_____ I tend to feel restless.

_____ When I have to sit still during meetings, classes, sermons, trips, etc., I tend to fidget (doodle, move my legs, do things with my hands, etc.).

_____ I tend to leave my seat when bored during long meetings or classes.

_____ I tend to want control of the channel changer when watching TV, whether alone or with others, and tend to flip channels to avoid boring advertisements or, simply out of curiosity, to know what is on multiple channels.

_____ I tend to be a multi-tasker (someone who, for example, might be watching a TV show and doing a crossword puzzle at the same time, or play video games while having a discussion with family or friends).

_____ I tend to hate to wait in lines for my turn in restaurants and other places.

_____ I tend to talk more than most of my friends when I am in a social situation.

IN SUMMARY

- Five or more in the first ten statements implies probable inherited attention deficit disorder, if lifelong.
- Five or more of the second ten statements implies probably inherited the hyperactivity component of the disorder, if lifelong.
- Five or more on both sets of ten implies ADHD (attention deficity hyperactivity disorder).

Chapter Eight

Mood Swing Blue Genes

The saddest case I've ever seen involved a bipolar college student who was a friend of mine. "Sally" had been a beautiful, straight-A, high school student who was a popular cheerleader and a professing Christian. Sally suffered a few depression episodes in high school, then had her first manic episode during her freshman year of college.

Sally lost her virginity during this manic period, which is common because the mania often drives a person to crave sex with whoever happens to be available. Two months later she found out she was pregnant. This devastating blow sent her into a depression racked with so much false guilt that she wrote a suicide note.

Usually, when we sin, it is because we choose to. So it seems logical to blame ourselves for sinful behavior—such as Sally's—committed when our brains act like a computer that shuts down for a while, though we would never do those things with the proper power steering fluids (serotonin, norepinephrine, dopamine and GABA).

I was a psychiatric resident at the time and on call in the psychiatric ER on a Sunday night when the police brought Sally in. Her parents had found her suicide note and called the police when she refused to go to the hospital.

For the first two hours she demanded to go home and refused to talk to us. I finally gave her the choice of voluntary admission or being committed against her will since she was an imminent danger to herself. She chose to stay voluntarily and then even admitted she wanted help. I started her on a medication, then grabbed an hour of sleep before morning rounds.

The next morning, the attending psychiatrist was angry with me for putting a pregnant woman on psychiatric medication, though the medicine I gave her is often used during pregnancy and is quite safe overall. He wouldn't even allow me to state my case, refusing to put her on anything but herbal medication because, as he said, "I don't have time to mess with getting sued and having my malpractice insurance go up when that baby is born with a birth defect."

Sally was discharged on Friday afternoon without medicine, and without medicine, a bipolar has no control over the depth of despair triggered by brain chemical deficiencies. She drove to the town where the baby's father lived. When he came home that Saturday afternoon, he found she had taken her own life. The autopsy revealed she had been carrying twins. Sally had a twin brother who has never been the same since her suicide, and both of her parents have also battled guilt and depression since then.

I finished my residency and moved before the legal case surrounding Sally's death was ever resolved. I'm sure that professor lived his worst nightmare—testifying and defending his treatment plan, while secretly wondering if he could have saved her life.

— TODD CLEMENTS, M.D.

Five percent of the population experiences uncontrollable mood swings, as Sally did, ranging from infrequent and mild to constant and severe. Collectively, these varying degrees of genetic mood swings are named bipolar spectrum disorders.

An estimated 300 million people worldwide live with this condition. In the United States close to 15 million people are afflicted with these mood swings. These aren't just people in mental institutions or prisons, but people you work with, go to church with, or perhaps even live with. There is a good chance it could be your boss. Many CEOs and successful professionals have bipolar spectrum disorders.

Thousands of bipolar physicians, pastors and business executives have received treatment at our clinics. Most of them live joyful, productive lives, experience happy marriages and rear well-mannered children. The handful of bipolar patients who cannot function in society are those who refuse to take medication, have never been treated with the right medication or try to function as their own doctors by medicating with alcohol and drugs. Bipolar disorder should be an illness that you control, not one that controls you.

Bipolar disorder is heavily linked to genetics. Depressed females outnumber depressed males by at least two-to-one, maybe even three-to-one. Bipolar disorder is equal between the two sexes, which gives credence to genetic causes. Many bipolar patients have at least one parent or grandparent with bipolar. A patient's disclosure that grandma had a "nervous breakdown" is usually a clue that points to bipolar disorder.

The manic phase is still much less understood than the depression in bipolar disorder. Mania is similar to epilepsy, where overactivity in one part of the brain causes loss of consciousness. This overactivity can spread across the entire brain resulting in a "grand mal" seizure with rhythmic thrusting movements. Mania consists of diffuse areas of overactive brain cells, resulting in racing thoughts, increased energy and irritability. There are several brain chemicals involved. This is one reason why anti-seizure medicines help bipolar so well.

The diagnosis of bipolar disorder is both good news and bad news.

Start with the Good News

When people in our Day Program first hear the word *bipolar*—or the obsolete term *manic-depressive*—as a possible diagnosis, most are frightened at the thought of having a "mental illness." But many are actually relieved to know there is a reason for the roller-coaster ride of pain they have experienced. They are even more relieved when reassured that with the right medications, they can get off that roller coaster of "blue gene" mood swings.

When diagnosed, people usually ask, "Will I ever be normal again?"

A typical answer—"I hope not"—draws a look of fear and desperation until they are assured, "You can be better than normal!"

One morning in 2004, I saw three outpatients in a row for brief, three-month medication checks. These three men, who did not know each other, all had bipolar disorder. Each man took his medicine properly and saw his counselor monthly. All three men reported feeling great and enjoying life. All three had been very successful over the past decade or so since getting on the right bipolar meds. They were humble, loving husbands.

They were also very rich. Two of them were billionaires and the third was worth five hundred million. (This goes to show that money doesn't buy happiness—the man with 500 million was just as happy as the man with a billion!) Instead of it being a crutch, bipolar actually worked to their advantage.

Bipolar people are often highly energetic, getting twelve hours of work done in eight hours. They are also willing to take risks, a needed skill when building a financial empire. Each man, however, was consistent with his treatment plan so the risks were thought out and not foolish.

Two of these men, when they were younger and first diagnosed by me, stopped taking the medicines I gave them, because they felt great for about six straight months. This happens often. Patients think they are well and no longer need their medications, even though I told them strongly that they would need the meds the rest of their lives.

Both of them became manic and both spent over a million dollars in one day with uncontrollable spending and tipping; both then crashed and became suicidal. Having learned their lessons, both men have stayed on the meds for over a decade now and have succeeded greatly ever since.

—PAUL MEIER, M.D.

Bipolar people are often very successful, creative and energetic. History is filled with notable people we now surmise had bipolar disorder: leaders of countries, heads of state, royalty, actors, musicians, physicians (especially psychiatrists), newscasters, and sports stars.

If you are rich, famous and bipolar it's fashionable to write a biography about it and become even more rich and famous. Biographies from bipolars are much more entertaining than those of depressed people who don't tell wild stories about the bizarre things they did when they were having their highs.

Today we have better medicines than ever before in treating bipolar disorder. With Hollywood increasing public awareness of this disease and avid research on brain chemical abnormalities in bipolar there are some great new medications coming down the pipeline that should be here in the next five years.

THEN THERE IS THE BAD NEWS

The bad news about bipolar is that too many people are misdiagnosed or go undiagnosed. This leads to more suicides, more drug addictions and more unnecessarily ruined lives. Bipolar people have so much intelligence and creativity that improper treatment is a tragic waste.

Bipolar patients, especially when they are hypomanic (still in touch with reality but feeling grandiose, talking rapidly, pouring out creative ideas, suffering insomnia, flirting excessively, giving big tips, etc.) often do not want treatment. They ask, "If I'm feeling good, why do I need treatment?"

Many family members also fail to understand why we treat mania. A relative will say, "Hey, Bob has the most energy he's had in years and is friendly. Please don't take that away." We want patients to have energy and feel good, but hypomania can turn rapidly into full-blown mania (psychosis, uncontrolled spending of an entire life savings, hostility, sexual affairs, etc.). Manic people can make foolish, impulsive decisions that ruin lives.

After almost every mania or hypomania, there is a rapid crash into depression, with people often becoming suicidal. Some manics even kill their family members, then kill themselves, with no understanding about what they are doing or why they are doing it.

With such severe consequences, why would a bipolar patient want to refuse medications? The only reason is foolish pride—pride in being "self-sufficient," pride in not having a "mental illness." In all fairness, the hypo-manic or manic person is helplessly grandiose. His brain chemicals make him positive he is right and normal and everybody else is acting a little "crazy" by insinuating that there is something wrong with him. He would call the President of the United States (or try to) at three in the morning to prove to you that he is normal. He really cannot help it. His family may have to call the police to lock him up against his will unless he goes voluntarily, which he is unlikely to do.

A recent case involved a pro basketball player with a contract for millions, who played well on medication but would stop taking it because he didn't think it was "spiritual." He lost his career and went in and out of psychotic mania, in and out of state hospitals, and in and out of prison. He is a wonderful, gentle, loving Christian man when on medications, but he fights with police when manic and may eventually get himself killed or kill himself.

This man wanted God to heal him, and God did—through our staff and our great new medications—but he didn't want God to do it that way. He wanted God to wave a magic wand and make it easy. He felt entitled to tell God how He should do it. In the process, he also lost his wife and children.

Another patient has worked three jobs for over two years to pay off a debt she incurred in one afternoon while manic. She drove by a beauty salon for sale and thought, "I'd like to be a hairstylist." She called her best girlfriend, a beautician, and asked, "If I bought a salon would you work for me and teach me to style hair?" Her friend agreed.

This patient then called a friend who was a loan officer at a bank and asked for a loan to buy the beauty salon. He foolishly agreed. She next asked the elderly couple selling the place to tell her the price—and then she bought it.

The elderly couple intentionally forgot to mention that the Department of Transportation was about to undertake a year-long widening project on that strip of road, and it would be closed to everyone except local traffic. Needless to say, her beauty parlor totally bombed.

This is just one example of how the manic phase can affect a person's behavior. While bipolars seldom kill themselves during the manic phase, they often do in the depressive dip that follows. Manic people may die, usually in accidents caused by their own careless decisions. Mania can make a person feel invincible.

Mania is like taking drugs—just because it feels good doesn't mean it is good for you. Hypomania can be very enjoyable and productive, but as it continues, it crosses over the line into full-blown mania, which is counterproductive.

BEYOND GENETIC CAUSES

Are mood swings always genetic or can they also be psychological or spiritual? The majority of depressive mood swings are due to a combination of spiritual and emotional factors on top of genetic influences.

Most people don't get depressed when everything is going well, but rather when a major stressor or tragedy occurs. Unresolved tragedy turns into bitterness, which then becomes a spiritual problem. Unresolved anger creates emotional problems as well. Learning to deal with tragedy and anger through forgiveness and growth brings about increased maturity and wards off depression.

Unresolved anger can actually result in serotonin depletion in the brain, thus leading to depression. This is an example of a biochemical problem, triggered by an emotional problem that was brought on originally by a spiritual problem. As the depression progresses, suicidal thoughts become more prominent.

Depression is more complicated than just chemical abnormalities. It involves physical aspects, emotional aspects and spiritual aspects. Medications are very helpful in improving the physical aspects (sleep, energy, sex drive, concentration, appetite), which then allows that person to start breaking the cycle of depression. Counseling enables people to learn how to confront and deal with the emotional and spiritual aspects of depression. Our society today, and Christian society in general, still has a difficult time accepting the fact that chemical abnormalities in certain parts of the brain can have physical, emotional and, especially, spiritual effects.

RELATIVES OF BIPOLAR DISORDER

Many bipolars have had lifelong ADHD, which was described in the previous chapter as either a detriment or an advantage. ADHD is a genetic "cousin" of bipolar disorder.

Thyroid abnormalities can also mimic bipolar disorder and ADHD. Getting a thorough physical exam (with thyroid labs included) yearly is very important. Thyroid problems are easily correctable, so it is unnecessary to suffer needlessly. An underactive or overactive thyroid can mimic bipolar. If your physician doesn't mention it, ask him to check your thyroid thoroughly. The tests we prefer for our day hospital patients are thyroid stimulating hormone (TSH), free T4, and free T3.

TREATMENT FOR BIPOLAR PATIENTS

Vitamins that contain the essential amino acids tryptophan, norepineph-rine, tyrosine and the essential nutrient choline, with Vitamin B6, are very helpful to build up the serotonin, norepinephrine, GABA and dopamine needed to prevent genetic mood swings, but vitamins alone are not enough.

All bipolar patients should be on a mood stabilizer, and some should also be on an antidepressant. Many bipolar patients can now get by just on Lamictil, or Geodon, or Abilify, or Seroquel. Keppra and Gabitril also look very promising. New ones will come out almost every year from now on as medical knowledge zooms into the future faster than most doctors can keep pace.

If a new client has bipolar, we will start with a mood stabilizer first, and if the depression also goes away, he or she can be sent home on just the one medicine. But we actually prefer to add the antidepressant, Wellbutrin-XL, as a precaution, since it rarely causes mania, and it prevents depression from coming back, increases energy, helps focus and concentration, helps ADHD, increases sexual enjoyment in the marital relationship without increasing temptations, and may cause weight loss at the same time.

If the person becomes manic while on a mood stabilizer, then a second, usually stronger, mood stabilizer is added. Using any serotonin anti-depressant when not needed in bipolar disorder can actually destabilize the mood, making it cycle up and down more rapidly.

Some bipolars still have severe, suicidal dips, even on a mood stabilizer, so we add an antidepressant, with Wellbutrin-XL being the first choice. If the patient has side effects on Wellbutrin-XL, such as excessive shakiness, then we go to one of the more risky serotonin antidepressants.

If a new patient arrives who is manic and even psychotic, we can use powerful but safe and nonaddicting medicines to get rid of the mania and the psychosis within a few hours to a few weeks. But the antidepressants work more slowly. They take an average of ten weeks to reach a peak affect. So the bipolar patient will feel relaxed and in touch with reality and have no more racing thoughts or severe anxiety or insomnia within a week or two of starting treatment, in most cases. But the sadness itself usually gets about ten percent better each week for ten weeks.

Most patients are able to go home and back to work within three weeks, because they no longer feel suicidal, just somewhat sad still. After ten weeks, 75 percent of them come back and report that this is the best they have ever felt in their lives, or at least in many years.

We do research on all of our Meier Clinic Day Program patients, measuring their level of symptoms when they come in and repeating the same questions when they go home three weeks later. The average for the past several years is a significant improvement in every area, with a 50 percent improvement in sadness level, after two to three weeks of treatment. If they were only receiving meds, there would only be a 30 percent improvement in sadness level after three weeks, but the education and group therapies and individual therapy all help improve their mood as well.

Often patients are referred who have been started on an antidepressant for depression but subsequently worsen. The antidepressant can make them irritable, restless, nervous and unable to sleep. Sometimes they become full of energy, euphoric, impulsive and grandiose. Antidepressants work well on the vast majority of people who need them. But if a person has bipolar relatives or has some bipolar spectrum tendencies in his or her genes from "somewhere back there" in the family history, then instead of working well, the antidepressants usually will either not work, or else precipitate a manic or hypomanic (milder than manic) episode.

If a mood stabilizer is added to the antidepressant, it will usually also work well for the bipolar patient. But if the patient is excessively manic, we will stop his antidepressants for a while, stabilize him on a mood stabilizer, then consider whether an antidepressant is needed or not.

If it is, a non-serotonin antidepressant, like Wellbutrin-XL, should be tried first for ten whole weeks, unless there are side effects. It will stop depression about 75 percent of the time. If it doesn't, then we will try the serotonin meds.

Anyone who gets manic or hypomanic on a serotonin antidepressant is almost certainly bipolar. The bipolar aspects of their illness just have never shown up yet. If someone inherits a bipolar spectrum disorder, it usually shows up a third of the time each in the teens, twenties or thirties. But some children exhibit it and some elderly get it for the first time, although this is rare. It is imperative for any type of doctor who is considering prescribing a medication for depression to take a comprehensive family history. Treating the wrong condition can wreak havoc.

Antidepressants sometimes get negative coverage in newspapers, magazines, and untrustworthy sources on the Internet. But the truth is, they have saved millions of lives. If you took a million people who are suicidal and gave them all a good, new antidepressant, ten weeks later 75 percent of them would be significantly improved. The other 25 percent could get that way too but will need to try a second antidepressant. There would probably be a few hundred people out of the million who commit suicide in spite of the antidepressant.

The partial truth to the hysterical stories in the press about antidepressants is that, in the five percent of the population who inherit bipolar spectrum tendencies, and in the one percent who inherit schizophrenia, if the doctor is not aware of this in their genetic makeup, those patients may very well become hypomanic, manic, or even psychotic on antidepressants if mood stabilizing meds are not given with them. Some of those people may commit suicide as a result of the worsened condition caused by the antidepressant. That is the true picture.

Types of Mood Swing Disorders

There are several types of mood disorders with ample evidence of genetic transmission from one generation to the next. The following summary describes each one in depth.

Dysthymia. This is a chronic, intermittent, low-grade depression. It doesn't meet all the criteria for major depression, but under stress it often progresses to a full-blown depression. Sufferers are negative, pessimistic people who find little joy in life and like to complain about everything.

If you gave a dysthymic person a million dollars in ten dollar bills, he would likely complain that you didn't use twenties. They rarely have suicidal ideation. They often deny anything is wrong with them and would consider themselves completely normal.

Dysthymic patients can be treated in therapy for years by the best counselors in the world and still not improve. The dysthymic person and the therapist sometimes both feel like failures. Antidepressants usually help improve their mood and demeanor somewhat, but these people still remain pessimistic.

The dysthymic person will often claim the medicine has not helped at all, but those who live and work with him will promise you that it has helped. Sometimes adding a GABA medicine will help calm and mellow out these critical and demanding personality types.

Dysthymic people can also exhibit mild paranoia, thinking that everybody is out to hurt them. In these cases a low dose of an atypical antipsychotic often improves their mood and allows them to trust others more.

New studies today reveal genetic transmission of dysthymia. On the other hand, some specialists claim that dysthymia is more due to environment, especially an unhappy childhood. This argument reasons that children raised by pessimistic parents learn that behavior. There is definitely truth to this, but studies involving identical twins who were reared in separate households support the genetic transmission theory.

As we have said earlier, who we are is made up of a combination of genetics, environment and life choices. Dysthymia—though not as serious as major depression— can still have damaging life consequences. Dysthymic people are more likely to be divorced (sometimes several times), have distant relationships with adult children and report loneliness and few friends.

Sometimes treating dysthymia can have amazing results and unveil a totally new, happy person who is fun to be around. This is what makes the long years of medical school and residency training worth every minute!

Unipolar Depression. These people experience the low periods, but not the highs of bipolar. Between bouts of depression they feel fine and function well. Some people experience one or two bouts of depression their whole lives, others experience one a year, and some suffer with several bouts of depression every year. Depression episodes are different for each person. Some people can't sleep; others want to sleep all of the time. Most people lose their appetite during depression, but a minority experience an increase in appetite.

Almost everyone reports low energy and poor concentration during depression. Some people are overcome with feelings of guilt, often over minor incidents. Depressed people also lose interest in the activities they used to enjoy. They also begin isolating from friends and family. This isolation worsens the cycle of depression because this person who already feels lonely now is even lonelier.

Thoughts about suicide are common in depression. Christians are not immune by any means to suicidal thoughts. These thoughts often create tremendous guilt in depressed Christians, because they know deep inside that is not God's plan for them.

It is important to distinguish which type of suicidal thoughts the person is having. Passive suicidality is thinking, "I don't want to kill myself, but I sure wouldn't mind if God took me home tonight." Some people passively kill themselves; for instance, someone with heart disease quits taking his medicine so he will die more quickly.

In his mind this is technically not suicide. Active suicidality is having a plan and intending to do it. When depression progresses to this point, the person should be hospitalized for his own safety. There is a myth that if you ask someone if they are suicidal, it will make them more likely to commit suicide. Actually, the opposite is true. The more that person can talk about it, the less likely he is to commit suicide.

Suicide threats are usually a cry for help or a form of manipulation. Sadly, some people use suicide threats for manipulation. We see several patients in our Day Program each year who stay in horrible relationships because the other partner has threatened to kill himself/herself if that person leaves.

Studies of identical twins reared apart show that if one twin has depression, the other twin has a 70 percent chance of having depression. The offspring of an adult with depression has a three-fold increased risk of developing a mood disorder compared to the general population.

Genetic factors have been estimated to account for 50 percent of depressions, while environmental factors and life choices account for 50 percent. In most people all three factors play a role. The earlier the age of onset of a mood disorder, the bigger role "blue genes" are thought to play. Children who develop depression almost always have a strong genetic component influencing it.

The elderly frequently suffer depression and are at risk for being misdiagnosed. Depression in the elderly often looks like dementia. It is so common, the term for it is "pseudodementia." There are numerous stories of elderly depressed people who were diagnosed with Alzheimer's dementia and put in a nursing home. When treated for depression, they returned to their old selves.

Anyone suspected of having dementia should be screened thoroughly for depression. If in doubt, treat them with an antidepressant.

I made this mistake on my own dear mother. When she was 88 years old, she quit taking her antidepressant without telling me or any other family members and quickly spiraled down into depression and senility. And I am very embarrassed to admit that I couldn't even tell she was depressed.

I honestly assumed she must have had multiple small infarcts (like mini-strokes) in her brain. My brother, sisters and I decided to move her from her apartment, where she lived alone and took care of herself quite well up to that point, and put her in a nursing home nearby, where we could all go visit her once a week each.

It was actually her family physician who asked my mom if she was still taking her antidepressant. My mom said she didn't think she needed it anymore, in spite of the obvious fact that off of it she was falling down, more forgetful, more confused, more irritable, and definitely sadder.

Her doctor restarted the medicine and within a few weeks she was back to normal. Today she is 96 years old and finally does need to live in assisted living, but she is still as sharp as a tack—sharp enough to still beat me in dominoes. With her antidepressant she is love in motion. Whenever I leave from a visit, she gives me a big hug, and then when I get out the door she calls me back to get one more. I am convinced that without her antidepressant, she would have died nearly a decade ago of "senility."

—Paul Meier, M.D.

Bipolar II. These people swing into three emotional states: 1) depressed, 2) normal, 3) hypomanic. Hypomania consists of manic symptoms such as racing thoughts, irritability, decreased need for sleep, increased activity, faster talking and increased impulsive behavior (often in the areas of spending or flirting). There is no psychosis in hypomania or loss of reality. Hypomanic states usually last at least four days, but less than a week. But we see quite a few patients with "atypical bipolar disorder" who have one or two day hypomanic episodes followed by crashes.

Someone who experiences more than four highs or lows combined per year is considered to be a "rapid cycler." Sometimes the high periods feel great, or euphoric, but sometimes they are not enjoyable or known as dysphoric. Some people experience a form of bipolar called "mixed episodes." These people experience both symptoms of hypomania and depression at the same time. During a mixed episode the person is usually very irritable and agitated easily. Child and adolescent bipolar episodes often present this way.

The majority of people with bipolar II spend more time in depression than hypomania. The typical pattern is to swing up to hypomania for four to seven days, then crash into depression lasting several weeks to months. However, there are numerous exceptions to this pattern, and many people have unpredictable patterns. The manic episodes usually come on gradually. The person will begin needing about an hour less sleep each night and start feeling more energized. Severe suicidal depression can strike quickly after a high period. Patients refer to this as their crash.

Mood stabilizers work well in treating bipolar II. Newer mood stabilizers work on both depression and hypomania. Risperdal, Abilify and Geodon are mood stabilizers with an FDA-approved indication for bipolar mixed.

Bipolar I. This is the more severe form, where the person experiences a full-blown manic episode. Manic episodes last at least a week and are more extreme than hypomanic episodes. People often make very impulsive and irrational decisions, such as spending their whole life savings in one day. We had a manic Day Program patient who once bought a brand-new Jaguar during lunch break. Thankfully, Dr. Meier was able to persuade the dealership to take the car back.

Manic people can lose touch with reality and become delusional. These delusions are usually grandiose (i.e., "I'm God!"). A former patient who lived in another state with his parents and worked a menial job became manic and called our clinic one day to let us know he had quit his job and had decided to become a NASCAR driver. He wanted to know if the Meier

Clinics would donate several hundred thousand dollars to sponsor his car. Luckily his mother got him to the hospital before he did something stupid. We turned down the offer to fund his racing career, of course.

Hearing voices that aren't there (auditory hallucinations), and seeing things that aren't there (visual hallucinations) are also common in bipolar I. People can also experience tactile hallucinations (such as feeling bugs crawling all over their bodies) or olfactory hallucinations (such as smelling foul odors); however, these are much less common.

When people are manic the voices are usually complimentary and ego-building; their visions will often consist of angels or God. When people are depressed, the voices are almost always derogatory and often tell people to do hurtful things to themselves or others. These are called "command hallucinations." Visions will be of demons, witches or dead people. Most hallucinations are mood "congruent," which means if depressed, they are negative and evil, and if manic, they are positive and spiritual.

Mood stabilizers are the main treatment in bipolar I.

MOOD STABILIZERS

Mood stabilizers fall into three categories. The first is *lithium*—the oldest mood stabilizer and still considered the "gold standard." It is used less and less today because it has many side effects, such as weight gain, sedation, fatigue, thirst, and so forth. Lithium is very deadly if the blood levels get too high. Patients who are on this medicine frequently have to have their blood drawn to check the lithium level because it is affected by many factors such as dehydration and other medicines. This adds expense and makes its use cumbersome for patients. Lithium can cause a heart defect known as "Ebstein's anomaly" if taken in the first trimester of pregnancy. The damage is usually already done before women on the medicine realize they are pregnant. Lithium can damage the thyroid gland as well. Lithium does not usually work very well on rapid cycling bipolar disorders, but usually works relatively well on slow cycling bipolar. Lithium also dulls the senses. Lithium is still used frequently in third world countries, state hospitals and prisons because it is very inexpensive.

The second category of mood stabilizers is *anticonvulsants.* Depakote and Tegretol were the first two used. They work well for rapid cycling bipolar. They too have many side effects: weight gain, liver damage, red blood cell damage, hair loss and fatigue. Blood levels have to be checked in these two as well. There is a new Depakote-ER that works well and has fewer side effects. Tegretol is troublesome to use because it speeds up the liver's ability to break down other medications. That means the person often has to increase the dose of all their other medications. Tegretol often makes birth control pills less effective. These two medicines can cause spinal cord formation abnormalities in a baby if taken by the mother while pregnant.

Newer anticonvulsants used are Lamictal, Trileptal, Topamax, Gabatril and Keppra. Topamax can cause weight loss (twenty pounds on average weight), which lots of our patients love, but it is not quite strong enough to be the only mood stabilizer for bipolar in most cases. It can cause kidney stones, but is often added as an adjunct medicine.

Lamictil is very good for mood stabilization and for depression, so it can be the only medication for many bipolars. These meds are much safer, and blood levels do not have to be checked. The anticonvulsants work on the GABA receptors. These medicines are especially helpful in a bipolar who has alcohol or drug addictions. Their action on the GABA receptor helps reduce the cravings for alcohol, marijuana, heroin and other narcotics. These meds also help anxiety, significantly reduce any chronic pain syndromes or headaches of any kind.

Atypical antipsychotics (now called psychotropics) are the newest class of mood stabilizers. Five of these are currently used for bipolar (Abilify, Geodon, Risperdal, Seroquel, and Zyprexa), and no doubt there will be more in the near future. These meds are quickly becoming the first line of treatment for bipolar for several reasons. They work on the serotonin and dopamine receptors, correcting the imbalances. They improve depression, protect from mania, and protect from psychosis (delusions and hallucinations). Auditory and visual hallucinations should be gone within a few days. This is important because psychotic people often follow their command hallucinations, which can end up in them hurting themselves or others. They also work quickly to eliminate mood swings (usually within a week). They can be given once a day, often at night, and relax the person for the next 24 hours. No blood levels have to be drawn either. Each one has a different side effect profile and we often use that to our advantage.

Zyprexa and Seroquel are the most sedating and have the most weight gain. They work best on manic patients who are not eating or sleeping adequately. Risperdal has less weight gain and is less sedating. It works well to calm those people who have high agitation levels. It can be taken during the day and will not "zonk" the person out. Geodon and Abilify are more stimulating and are weight neutral. They work well in depressed lethargic bipolars. They are good medications to use for those people who have to work, since they have very little sedation.

All of the antipsychotics can supposedly cause diabetes, so we monitor the blood sugar of patients while on the medication. We think that some of the antipsychotics cause significant weight gain, and when that occurs in middle-aged people, it can bring on adult onset diabetes. So the medicine itself may not cause diabetes at all, but the weight gain is probably what makes it appear to. The main complaint we hear about these medicines is that they cost about ten dollars a pill. The good news is that some of these should go generic in the next few years, which would dramatically lower the price.

GETTING HELP

If any of the conditions described in this chapter sounds like you, please see an M.D. (psychiatrist), and at least get an evaluation. If you realize your mate, child, sibling, parent, or friend is suffering from a bipolar spectrum disorder, please love that person enough to do what you can to persuade him or her to get help.

The most successful time to persuade a person is during a depressed phase. Usually people will resist help during a manic period. If he or she is an alcohol or drug addict, rehab to detox off of drugs will be needed first. We highly recommend a thirty-day stay at Calvary Ranch Rehab Center in Phoenix, Arizona. Call 1-888-7-CLINIC for more information.

With or without treatment, bipolar people have a one in five chance of committing suicide. Without treatment, it is much higher. That is a sad fact that families have to deal with every day.

Having psychological problems such as depression, bipolar, anxiety, or addictions does not mean these problems are a result of moral weakness or lack of will power. Poor moral choices can result in guilt, low self-esteem, fear of rejection, sexually transmitted diseases, negative impacts on the lives of others, depression, anxiety and addictions. But all of these can have genetic components—"blue genes"—as well. And bipolar is nearly totally genetic, regardless of spirituality.

Even in these cases it is not always the afflicted one with the moral lapse. If your spouse leaves you for another person, out of the blue, his or her moral failure can affect you.

The music minister at my former church had a father who died of a massive heart attack in his forties. He and his two brothers lived a healthy lifestyle and loved God. His two older brothers also died of heart attacks in their forties. He is now forty-one.

He exercises daily and eats very healthily, yet he knows heart trouble in his family is genetic, so he might not live to be fifty. Just as genetic influences can take down the heart of a man with a healthy lifestyle, a genetic influence can accentuate psychological problems in the most moral person you know.

If you are a Christian and feel that God shouldn't allow you to suffer any psychological problems, then quit wasting money on health insurance and throw away your vitamins and blood pressure medicine, because He shouldn't allow you to suffer these, either. Cannot God work through counselors and medicine to help with mental problems as well?

Blue gene problems are physical; they involve physical abnormalities with physical chemicals that strongly influence how and what you think, as well as how you feel about yourself, your life, others, and God. If you need psychiatric medications and do not have access to a Christian psychiatrist in your area, see a Christian counselor to deal with your issues, and see a non-Christian psychiatrist who is good at medications. Just don't ask him to discern spiritual matters with you. Or else travel to a good Christian psychiatrist and then have your family doctor follow up if the psych meds are not too complicated.

If you have a complicated "blue genes" problem, like bipolar or psychotic depression, do not go to your family doctor to decide what medications you should be on. See a psychiatrist. You wouldn't go to your family doctor for brain surgery, would you?

Family doctors are often fine if you know you don't have any bipolar or schizophrenic relatives and you have a simple depression. Most family doctors do not have the time to keep up with all the new psychiatric medicines, just as psychiatrists don't have time to keep up with all the latest meds for physical (non-brain) illnesses.

People with mood swing "blue genes" can live productive, normal lives. They can also serve God very faithfully. They do need support from friends, family, and their medical team. Don't ruin your potential because you are too proud to ask for help. There is great help available today. Living life with constant severe mood swings is needless with today's technology and medication!

Chapter Nine

Hormonal Blue Genes

"*This is Police Sergeant James. We have your son, Anthony, in our custody.*"

These words roused Jimmy Smith from his sleep at two in the morning as he answered the unexpected phone call.

"*Your son, Anthony, has been involved in a physical assault against a teenager from another high school. Neither boy is seriously injured. However, Anthony is under arrest, and since he is a minor, I need you to come down here and sign some papers before he can leave.*"

Jimmy knew Tony had been acting strangely the last few months, but the middle-of-the-night call was the first sign of a deep problem. Tony was irritable, argumentative and sometimes would stay awake the whole night, but Tony had always been a good son—honor roll grades, starter on the football team, and a leader in the church youth group. What had gone wrong? Was it drugs?

Jimmy called Whit Hawkins, the head football coach, the next morning to let him know what had happened and to see if he had noticed any strange behavior in Tony. Coach Hawkins admitted he and some of the assistant coaches were concerned that Tony had gained close to thirty pounds over the last two months. Currently the team was involved in off-season weight training, and Tony and two other players had greatly increased their strength and lost considerable body fat in a short amount of time. The assistant coaches had denied the suggestion of steroid use.

Coach Hawkins insisted, "We're always talking to the kids about the dangers of using steroids. We tell them steroids cause aggression, poor decision-making, depression, and sometimes even suicide. If Tony's on steroids, I'd hate to lose him as a player, but I would rather he learn his lesson now than die of liver cancer in his thirties."

"I wish every coach was like you and had more concern for their players' health than just winning," added Jimmy.

"And I wish every father got involved like you, Mr. Smith. Call me when you find out what's happening."

After a serious talk with his dad, Tony confessed he had been using anabolic steroids he and his teammates bought from a local body builder.

Thanks to an involved dad, Tony had learned his lesson early. Many high school boys and girls are not so fortunate, and are risking their health in a gamble to increase speed and physical strength.

Tony and others like him think nothing of tampering with the body's natural hormonal balance by using steroids. The physical, mental, and emotional consequences can be severe.

WHAT ARE HORMONES AND HOW DO THEY WORK?

Hormones are what make a man masculine and a woman feminine. Our bodies consist of hundreds of hormones that control or "oversee" thousands of bodily functions. Hormones affect everything from our skin softness to sex drive.

Hormones essentially are chemicals produced by different cells in the body that act as "communicators" carrying messages to and from all organs of the body. They connect one organ's function to another. They keep our bodies balanced and functioning optimally—and without them we would die.

These messengers carry out the commands of genes. Genes, for instance, determine at conception if we are male or female, but it is not until further along in the process, when hormones play their role, that the baby starts developing into a boy or girl. Hormones that go awry can look and act like "blue genes." Genes can also malfunction, wreaking havoc, by leaving part of the body under- or overresponsive to certain hormones.

Hormones are divided into two types—*protein hormones* and *steroid hormones.* We're going to look at thyroid hormone and three important steroid hormones: cortisol, estrogen and testosterone. These four are known to play a large role in managing mental well-being. Melatonin is a hormone that plays a lesser role, but abnormal levels can also affect moods.

Hormones are *extremely* powerful compounds. They are released into the bloodstream from their organ(s) of origination and work throughout the entire body. They are so potent that it often takes the release of less than a billionth of a gram for the hormone to exert its effect throughout the body! Many hormones have multiple jobs, exerting different effects in different organs. This makes regulating hormones an amazingly complicated process.

The pituitary gland historically is known as "the master gland" because it sends out hormones that influence all the other glands of the body. But now we know that another small gland in the brain bosses the pituitary around—the hypothalamus.

The hypothalamus even has a "satiety center" that influences our appetites. Dr. Meier had a patient years ago who was consistently happy, maintained a normal weight, and became a missionary to Central America. Then, for no apparent reason, she began putting on a lot of weight and becoming increasingly depressed, and eventually suicidal.

The other missionaries counseled her the best they could, but could find no reason for her suicidal urges and binge eating. She was five feet, two inches tall and went from 110 pounds all the way up to 317 pounds. Finally, they sent her to our clinic for treatment. Her physical exam and labs were normal, so we assumed her problems must be psychological or spiritual.

We dug and probed, looking for a root problem, but could come up with nothing. At last a brain scan revealed a tumor larger than an orange pressing on her hypothalamus, messing up her satiety center and causing her severe depression. We sent her to a neurosurgeon who successfully removed the tumor, and she rapidly recovered from her depression. Her weight gradually returned to normal.

Three separate structures, or "glands," regulate cortisol, also commonly known as the "stress hormone." The hypothalamus, the "true" master gland, is a small area deep within the brain. It secretes the substance (or pre-hormone) cortisol releasing factor (CRF).

CRF travels throughout the bloodstream and tells the pituitary gland to secrete cortisol releasing hormone (CRH). CRH then travels in the bloodstream and tells the adrenal glands (which are located on top of the kidneys) to release cortisol into the bloodstream. Cortisol is then released, which travels throughout the body and helps us with stress, healing and immunity.

Why God made our systems this complicated has intrigued scientists for centuries. Yet King David wrote (in Psalm 139) three thousand years ago that we humans are definitely fearfully and wonderfully designed by God, and "woven" in our mother's wombs as we were designed by Him.

How someone who has studied the vast complexity of hormones can come away not believing we have a creator is incomprehensible. There is absolutely no way such an elaborate system of checks and balances could have evolved.

If your understanding is limited to just the knowledge of how hormones work (ignoring the thousands of other vast, complex systems the human body uses to function), all four authors of this book still say that it takes mountains more faith to believe in atheism than in a Divine Designer. To think that this all bounced together out of nothing, as atheists believe, is almost psychotic, in our opinion.

We've been talking about brain chemical imbalances all through this book and how they contribute to psychiatric disorders. Now we're talking about how hormones play a role in moods too. How does that connect at all with brain chemicals? Good question. This is another area of medicine where we know there is a strong connection, but just aren't sure yet how everything is interwoven. We do have some pretty good ideas though.

We know that underactivity or overactivity in certain parts of the brain is responsible for psychiatric symptoms. These areas of abnormal activity are accompanied by brain chemical imbalances also.

Psychiatric medicine today focuses on restoring the balance of brain chemicals, which in turn can correct the abnormal area of activity. The question from the beginning, which still remains, is, "What causes these abnormalities in the first place?" Why do those who have them usually only have them part of the time, especially if it is genetic?

In other words if you have the "blue genes" for depression, why are you not depressed every single day? What enables you to go days, weeks, or perhaps months feeling good, without any treatment?

Hormones could be the key to this puzzle! Genetics are the basic underlying principle factors behind our body's makeup. We have explained in the first several chapters how inherited genes (that we call "blue genes") can cause disease and suffering. Genes can also malfunction, which usually results in that gene's function not being carried out.

Sickle cell anemia is a perfect example here. The gene malfunctions and the bone marrow (the organ that makes red blood cells) makes hemoglobin that causes misshapen blood cells (ones that look like sickle blades, rather than disc shaped cells, which look like Frisbees). Sickle shaped cells do not float through the blood vessels nearly as easily as Frisbee shaped cells, so when the percentage of sickle shaped cells in the blood gets too high, they start getting stuck in the smaller vessels. This causes organs and tissues to die from lack of oxygen and nutrients. It is also very painful.

Genes often carry out their functions through hormones, so imbalanced hormones could be the result of malfunctioning genes or faulty organs involved in regulating the hormones. Since many hormones are regulated by an axis (often consisting of more than one hormone), discovering where the breakdown is occurring can be very perplexing.

Hormones regulate bodily functions, which includes brain chemicals, so hormone irregularities can result in brain chemical abnormalities. There you have it; it's about as clear as mud. The truth is also that we're not sure which one is the cart and which one is the horse.

Think of the whole gene-hormone-neurotransmitter connection as your favorite professional football team. The gene is the team owner. It is his job to decide who the players will be for his particular team. The coach is the hormone. It is his job to regulate the players, telling them how to carry out the plays. The players are the neurotransmitters, or brain chemicals. They are the ones in the trenches actually getting the job done (or not).

Let's say a psychiatric disorder is a losing team (one not getting the job done). There could be several reasons for this: The owner failed to hire enough good players. It could be that he didn't have the money or means to hire good players (blue gene) or because he was an idiot (malfunctioning gene). Good players may have been on the team, but the coach didn't know how to stimulate them to play (hormonal problem). The problem could be the fault of the players. They could have several that are sick, injured, or under the influence of drugs (neurotransmitter imbalance).

The solution could be changing owners (gene replacement therapy), which is not here today but should be in the next five to ten years. More coaches could be added to help the existing coach (hormonal therapy). This might make things better or worse.

Solving the problem by starting with the players is another solution. Treating the sick, injured, and drug abusing players will definitely help them perform better, along with adding extra players to help carry the load (counseling and pharmacological therapy and improved nutrition— see chapter 10). Psychiatry today focuses on helping the players or coaches. We have had more success and also found that it is more predictable to treat the players.

Let's look at a real-life example: The limbic system is a small area deep in the brain, which plays a large role in regulating moods and emotions. Overactivity in the limbic system produces negative emotions, including sadness, irritability, agitation, and even anger. Taking a serotonin enhancing medication "calms down" an overactive limbic system, which brings back relaxation, peace, and joy.

Women who suffer with significant premenstrual syndrome (PMS) also show increased limbic system activity during the week of PMS symptoms. Many gynecologists think the drop in estrogen levels the week before menstruation causes PMS. Why it bothers some women and not others is still a mystery.

Giving estrogen to a female with PMS during that week of symptoms will relieve the symptoms. Estrogen also "calms down" the activity in the limbic system. Serotonin medications such as Sarafem (Prozac), Lexapro, or Zoloft relieve PMS symptoms as well.

Here's the billion-dollar question (that the pharmaceutical companies all want to have answered): Does an estrogen abnormality overactivate the limbic system, which in turn lowers serotonin in that part of the brain?

Or, does estrogen lower serotonin levels in the brain, which in turn overactivates the limbic system? Could it possibly be the other way around, whereby overactivity in the limbic system, or low brain serotonin levels, causes abnormalities in estrogen function? Researchers aren't sure what the answer is yet. It may be some combination of the three or even differ depending on the person.

The rest of this chapter contains a brief overview of a few of the hormones that affect mental functioning.

THYROID HORMONE: THE FUEL

The thyroid gland is a small unnoticeable organ in your neck sitting right under the Adam's apple. Think of the thyroid as your gas pedal. The thyroid controls the body's rate of metabolism. It does this specifically by increasing the body's use of oxygen and increasing heat production, which raises the rate we burn energy (calories). Think of thyroid hormone as the fuel. An overactive thyroid gland that releases elevated amounts of hormone is known as a state of "hyperthyroidism."

Hyperthyroidism has both signs and symptoms. Symptoms are what you feel. Signs are what others (such as your doctor) can outwardly see. Increased appetite would be a symptom (what you feel), whereas eating two buckets of fried chicken would be a sign (what I can see). Symptoms are nervousness; inability to sleep, which leads to fatigue; feeling hot and sweating, even at room temperature; a racing heart; weight loss despite increased appetite; agitation; emotional instability—crying one minute then laughing the next; shortness of breath; and diarrhea. Signs are trembling, especially in the hands; constant red sweaty palms; abnormally fast heartbeat, sometimes skipping beats; enlarged thyroid gland; skin flushing; and nausea and vomiting. If insomnia continues, a state of delirium can develop.

Hyperthyroidism can look like severe anxiety or a manic episode. The thyroid is called the "great imitator" because abnormalities in this gland can look like virtually any psychiatric illness. People with untreated hyperthyroidism can easily die of a heart attack or stroke. Continually beating too fast can eventually wear the heart down.

If thyroid hormones control the body's rate of burning calories, could you help people lose weight by giving them thyroid hormone? The answer is yes. But artificially putting someone in a hyperthyroid state is too dangerous. The risk for heart attack and stroke is too high. People can also become psychotic when they are hyperthyroid (this is usually in the form of paranoia). Chronic hyperthyroidism can cause exopthalmos (a condition where your eyes "bug out"). If your thyroid is normal and a health professional ever suggests turning it up to lose weight, even if it is only for a short time—run! Run all the way to your car, lock the doors, and squeal your tires to get out of there as fast as you can. Being thin is not worth it when you are dead from a heart attack or paralyzed from a stroke.

Underactive thyroid, or hypothyroidism, is what we see the most in psychiatry. Hypothyroidism often imitates depression. Women develop hypothyroidism 10-20 times more often than men do. Low thyroid can mean problems with the thyroid gland, pituitary gland, or hypothalamus. Sometimes psychiatric medications, such as lithium, can slow down the thyroid gland. Hypothyroidism can also mimic bipolar disorder. Sixty percent of people with rapid cycling type II bipolar disorder have low thyroid function.

Symptoms of hypothyroidism are: constant tiredness; feeling cold all of the time; gaining weight, even though your appetite is low; hair loss; irregular menstrual periods; achy muscles and joints; constipation; depressed mood, or rapid mood swings; and memory impairment, sometimes to the point of a dementia-like state. Signs are: dry, flaky skin; coarse hair and brittle nails; water retention—puffy face and hands; hoarse voice; slow heart rate; and an orange-ish hue to the skin.

Untreated hypothyroidism often leads to a suicidal depression that is profoundly lethal. In other words, these people are not playing around or trying to get attention by attempting suicide—they are bent on killing themselves and often succeed. It can also cause psychosis in some instances. If only the depression is treated, without correcting the underlying thyroid abnormality, there is usually only a minimal response to antidepressants and/or counseling. This is a situation where both the thyroid levels and the mood problems need to be treated. Thyroid levels can be measured with a blood test. Hypothyroidism can be treated quite easily (compared to other hormonal problems) by adding thyroid hormone, which comes in a pill form. Anyone over eighteen years old who visits a physician for mood problems should have his or her thyroid checked.

There are also "natural" methods to treat hypothyroidism, advertised by herbalists and "organic pharmacies." None of these methods are proven to work. A few of them might, but most of the ones we've seen don't. With the propensity of those suffering for suicide and psychosis, hypothyroidism is nothing to mess around with, especially given the fact that thyroid hormone works. How is taking a bottle of unknown ingredients in a pill form more "natural" than taking the actual hormone in a pill form?

As suggested before—pharmaceutical companies did not become multi-billion dollar companies by being stupid. They know about all the different herbs out there and surely have tested every one of them. If something works consistently, they are going to find a way to patent it, get it FDA approved, and sell it to the public.

CORTISOL: THE STRESS HORMONE

Cortisol is the "stress" hormone. It is made by the adrenal glands, which sit on top of the kidneys. Psychiatrists have had the ability to study the effects of abnormal cortisol levels for over half a century. Tuberculosis (TB) was formerly the most common cause of adrenal failure, which led to cortisol deficiency. Tuberculosis was rampant in mental hospitals during the first half of the twentieth century due to overcrowding and poor sanitation. Efforts to restore cortisol were crude, which left many patients with elevated cortisol levels.

Cortisol is thought to play a role in depression, anxiety, OCD, anorexia, chronic fatigue syndrome, psychosis, substance abuse, and sleep. High cortisol levels are presumed to precipitate mood disturbances. Our body releases extra cortisol when we are under high stress, as it physiologically prepares us to deal with any upcoming distressing event.

The current predominating theory is that a significant number of people who suffer from depression have adrenal glands that release excessive amounts of cortisol when they are stressed. This makes sense when you consider the fact that most people don't have mood problems when life is smooth, but rather when it becomes stressful. Life today is probably more stressful than at any other time on earth (except when dinosaurs chased people around). Could this be a major factor in why depression is so prevalent in our generation? Probably so. Stress today seems inescapable!

Interestingly, successfully treating depressed individuals with noted abnormal cortisol levels almost always normalizes their cortisol function. This is one hormone where it works better to treat the players rather than the coach. GABA medications work particularly well in depression associated with elevated cortisol. This is probably due to their ability to calm and relieve stress, which in turn reduces the cortisol release.

The relief gained from GABA enhancing meds also helps explain the link with substance abuse. These people are probably more prone to abusing "downers" like alcohol, Xanax, Valium, muscle relaxers, and even marijuana, because they hit the GABA receptors and relieve stress. Pharmaceutical companies have known about the cortisol/mood connection for years and have been trying to create an antidepressant that directly affects cortisol. So far nothing has successfully made it through clinical trials. What I've heard (from drug reps who spoke "off the record") is that most companies are now focusing on creating more powerful and more specific GABA meds.

Chronic high cortisol levels result in Cushing's syndrome. If the problem is in the adrenal glands or because a person is taking steroid medication, it is Cushing's syndrome (not Cushing's disease, which is different).

People with Cushing's have a certain look—central obesity (pot belly); a round "moon" face; a "buffalo hump" fat pad on the back of the neck; and usually skinny arms and legs. What if that just happens to be what the patient looks like? We have our patients bring in pictures of themselves dating back at least five years. If they look totally different, then we can diagnose Cushing's before even doing the test.

People with Cushing's have mood disturbances more than 50 percent of the time, with over 10 percent reporting severe suicidal thoughts. Psychosis is common too. Cushing's patients are also known to have severe cognitive impairments, sometimes to the point of dementia. Abnormal cortisol is thought to play a role in the concentration and memory problems seen in depression. It also explains why many of us have a difficult time performing complex tasks under stress—our memory and concentration worsen.

Too little cortisol results in Addison's disease. President John F. Kennedy suffered from Addison's disease. Addison's results in severe fatigue, apathy, impaired sleep, and depressed moods. If not treated with cortisol, these people will die.

Some physicians and herbalists are treating mood problems and other disorders with cortisol or some other form of steroids. This again is dangerous, not proven to work, and seems like it would worsen mood problems rather than improve them. Anyone requiring cortisone treatment should be under the care of an endrocrinologist, as this is the proper area of expertise.

TESTOSTERONE: IT'S A GUY THING

Both men and women make testosterone, though women have a minisculc amount compared to men. Testosterone has long been known to have mood lifting properties, but too much is harmful. Here is another hormonal example of a double-edged sword, so testosterone replacement treatment must be undertaken cautiously.

Testosterone controls male sexual development and oversees the making of sperm. It enhances the libido in both men and women. It also promotes muscle growth, which makes it a target of abuse by athletes, as steroids, to gain a competitive edge. Too much testosterone causes acne, irritability, aggression, and hypersexuality. Women with too much testosterone start looking like men with dark facial hair growth and deepening voices. Chronic elevated testosterone leads to testicular and prostate cancer.

Administering high levels of testosterone to animals increases their violent behavior. There is some thought that men with high levels of testosterone are more prone to commit sexual and violent crimes.

There have been studies done on prison populations, which showed that an increased percentage of prisoners, compared to the general population, had elevated testosterone levels. There have actually been some notorious criminals who have been found to have an extra Y chromosome, which would result in high testosterone levels.

We check for elevated testosterone levels when men come in who have started having anger problems, especially if that is not their normal personality. An example is one patient in our Day Program who worked as an administrator for an international ministry organization. His wife described him as loving and gentle until the last year and a half. He had become explosive, where even minor conflicts led to screaming, yelling, and even threatening. He had developed severe road rage, which is not a great characteristic when you are driving one of the ministry's vans. She felt he was always "on the edge."

The patient described an inability to sleep, which left him feeling strung out the next day. He also had a huge appetite and had gained almost 50 pounds. He told another physician previously about his racing thoughts and had been put on medicine for bipolar disorder. It helped a little.

He was in his late 40s and had never had an episode like this before, nor had he ever been depressed, so we didn't think it was bipolar disorder. He noticed only a slight difference after several months on the medication. His wife was at her wit's end. She was now scared he might physically hurt her, but she didn't want to divorce him because it would ruin his career and cause a scandal in the ministry.

His testosterone level was quite high. After further questioning he remembered to tell us that he had seen a doctor over a year ago because he was feeling fatigued. This doctor told him he had too much estrogen and prescribed him some kind of cream that came in a white tube from a local compounding pharmacy.

He never went back to see the doctor because he thought he might be a quack (sounds like he was), but he thought that cream did help his energy level so he kept taking it. When he ran out, he called the doctor's office and got refills. We called the compounding pharmacy and sure enough—it was testosterone cream. Luckily, his condition was simple to treat: we just threw that white tube in the trash.

Low testosterone (known as hypogonadism) is a much more common occurrence among adults—in both males and females. Up to one-third of men over age fifty are believed to have low testosterone levels. Only a very small percentage of these men are receiving treatment.

I wonder how many millions of men there are in America today who are walking around tired, depressed, with low interest in sex—even with Viagra—looking at the world negatively, and maybe even wondering what's left in their lives. Many of them may even be on antidepressants that are only providing minimal help, which is often even more depressing.

Symptoms of low testosterone are chronic fatigue, which resembles low motivation or apathy; decreased interest in sex, which can reach the point of sexual dysfunction; and decreased muscle mass. New research also shows that men with testosterone deficits exhibit memory problems.

They can grasp new information, but they cannot remember it for very long. This new finding hints at why forgetfulness plagues older men. Men with lower testosterone levels are often less dominating and behave more submissively.

Why are we seeing such a huge number of men with hypogonadism? One theory being debated is that the testosterone levels of men are lowered with each successive generation. The reasoning is that men with the highest testosterone levels are more prone to violence and hence are more likely to die or be imprisoned before producing children.

Young men attracted to military service are also those with higher testosterone levels (this is according to the unproven theory) and have an increased risk of getting killed prior to fathering. That leaves us low testosterone guys around to do all the reproducing, so our boys will genetically possess low testosterone levels.

This theory also espouses that women are moving, generation to generation, toward higher testosterone production. Women with higher testosterone levels are thought to be more assertive, which is an advantage in today's society. These women supposedly become the leaders. Supporting evidence is that girls are more aggressive in courting boys today, that women are more promiscuous than ever before, and that females have caught up with males in the rates of infidelity in marriage.

According to this theory, after a few more generations, there will be very little difference between males and females. Not likely. Young men have been killed in war for thousands of years and men haven't turned into women yet.

Why do so many men have low testosterone? It probably has a lot to do with the fact we are living longer. One hundred years ago the average life span was less than fifty years so this was less of a problem, and nobody could measure testosterone anyway.

I don't think we even knew what it was. Prostate surgery can reduce testosterone, along with many medications used today. The more appropriate question is, "Why aren't we doing more about it?" This is treatable.

Supplementing testosterone in hypogonadism improves mood, increases energy, reduces irritability, heightens sexual desire and function, and increases muscle mass. Adding testosterone to men who have normal levels has less proven benefit.

Physicians have finally listened to women who complain of low libido and energy and are developing a testosterone replacement patch for women that should be on the market soon (at the time of this writing the FDA continues to hold up the process). We have long known that adding small amounts of testosterone to postmenopausal women is beneficial.

The growing numbers of female physicians finally brought this issue to the forefront. Jill Warnock, M.D., and Elizabeth Vliet, M.D., two noted female psychiatrists specializing in women's mental health issues, have been instrumental in this, with their vocal support of providing women this treatment option.

If you are experiencing these symptoms, ask your doctor to check your testosterone level. It can be done with a simple blood test (there are weird hair and saliva tests available, but blood is the most reliable). One important point—testosterone levels are highest in the morning and then drop throughout the day (as much as 50 percent). If you have your levels drawn early in the morning it might show up normal when it's really not. An optimal time to have the level drawn is right after lunch. This tells the doctor approximately where the midpoint is.

Rubbing a gel on your shoulders and arms can replace testosterone, or using a patch, which sticks to the buttocks, or biweekly injections. Rubbing the gel on after you take a shower in the morning closely resembles the body's natural cycle.

The patches are cumbersome and patients complain they fall off every time they pull their pants down. The injection has been popular because it's cheap and easy, but it can cause symptoms of elevated testosterone the first week or so and the levels can dwindle before the next injection. It's also difficult to know just when to re-measure the testosterone level after an injection to get the truest reading.

There are advertisements everywhere for herbs claiming to increase sexual desire and stamina. If your testosterone levels are low, these are probably a waste of money—treat testosterone deficiency with testosterone. What's more "natural" than that? Some people also buy DHEA (another testosterone-like hormone) from the nutrition stores. This can mess up the testosterone level in a big way.

One last point involves the steroid usage described in the story opening this chapter. Many high school boys admit they take steroids to get an edge in sports. Some young adult bodybuilders also take steroids to enhance their muscle growth. Steroids consist of testosterone or a substance similar to it. When you mess with God's design in this way, the results can be devastating.

There have been cases of steroid rage, where the person becomes highly aggressive. There have been cases of mania and psychosis leading to involuntary inpatient treatment in a mental hospital for otherwise normal teens, an incident that will be on record for the rest of their lives. There have been unexplained heart failures in young men, problems thought to be connected with steroid use. But what we are seeing in psychiatry, and is most alarming, is suicide. Taking a large dose of steroids tricks the brain into putting the brakes on the testes (the organ responsible for making testosterone). When the steroid dose wears off, testosterone levels drop rapidly because the testicles are still on vacation. This often brings on depression, severe irritability, and suicidal thoughts. Sadly, some carry through with it. Taking repeated doses of steroids can also leave a man impotent, whereby he can never have children. Is the benefit worth the risk? No.

DHEA: Fountain of Youth or Snake Oil?

Recent news reports have called DHEA "the mother of all hormones." On the Internet it has even been billed as a "fountain of youth." It is being touted as a panacea that prevents cancer, helps us live longer, reduces heart disease and Alzheimer's disease, and combats against AIDS and other infections.

Other physicians refer to DHEA as the "snake oil of the twenty-first century." There are some controversial studies that show DHEA can reduce depression in a small percentage of middle-aged men. This is in large part thought to be due to its effects of raising testosterone levels. There is also a scant amount of evidence showing it to boost the immune system in older adults.

The truth is we really know very little about DHEA or what effect it has on our bodies; it has the potential to both raise and lower testosterone levels. The Food and Drug Administration is not sure what to do with DHEA supplements either, which right now are sold over the counter. Many researchers think of it as a kind of "chemical trash" left over as a breakdown product from other hormones. It is very similar to both estrogen and testosterone, so what it does put into the body is very unpredictable. There have been studies which link it to heart disease in women, sterility, high cholesterol, and stimulation of the growth of prostate tumors. There have also been cases noted in the last few years linking DHEA use to heart-rhythm disturbances, acne, hair loss, menstrual irregularities, irritability, and aggression.

There are really no proven benefits of taking DHEA, yet the potential for irreversible side effects is real.

ESTROGEN: IT'S A GIRL THING

Estrogen is very complicated and affects so many organ systems it would take a book the size of an encyclopedia to explain it. There is also the controversy surrounding hormone replacement with estrogen. If we were to tell you today's recommendations for when and how to use estrogen replacement, those recommendations would be changed by the time this book goes to print. The changes happen so quickly, even the Internet can barely keep up. We're going to focus on the role estrogen plays in mental health.

Women have many more sex hormones than men. The larger number of hormones also means there is a greater chance for genetic malfunctioning or "blue genes." Some have hypothesized that this is why women outnumber men two to one in depression.

Estrogen, which is made by the ovaries, can influence activity in the limbic system as we mentioned earlier. The better question regarding estrogen is, "What does it not play a role in?" The answer is probably, "Nothing." Estrogen is thought to alter the activity of serotonin, dopamine, and norepinephrine. Through these pathways, estrogen affects mood, sleep, pain, appetite, sex drive and memory. Estrogen itself is thought to have mood-enhancing properties.

As we unravel more intricate details concerning estrogen, leading physicians are now theorizing that it is not the actual level of estrogen in the bloodstream that is so important, but rather the ratio of estrogen to other sex hormones, the most notable one being progesterone. Progesterone is also produced by the ovaries and is similar to estrogen. Progesterone increases GABA, which reduces anxiety and promotes sleep.

Estrogen and progesterone work together in providing normal function. Their levels are constantly fluctuating so at any given time one is dominant. When estrogen is dominant the body is said to be in an "estrogenic" state, and a "progestrogenic" state when progesterone dominates.

Mental well-being seems to do better in an "estrogenic" state. Women's mental health specialists talk about estrogen to progesterone rations (E:P). Mood disorders often improve if the E:P ratio is at least 2:1. Researchers for years have looked at using estrogen alone as an antidepressant, but now focus on proper E:P balance. Estrogen may be the strongest mood-modulating hormone in our body. Men have estrogen too, but in small amounts.

As the life expectancy continues to rise, women will be living more years after menopause, and this means the question of hormone replacement is here to stay. The research results are confusing because estrogen affects almost everything. Now when you ask about hormone replacement the doctor says, "Well it will lower your risk of A, B, and C; but it will increase your risk of D, E, and F." So what do you do? Become your own expert in this field! How? Read. We will recommend resources and suggest you read medical articles concerning this as well. But the first rule is to stay away from *any* magazine in the grocery store giving medical advice!

The second rule is to be very careful on the Internet. Search well-known and respected sites such as WebMD.com. Scrutinize the author of anything you read. What are his credentials? Is he associated with a university? You can actually become quite knowledgeable this way.

When you feel you have a solid grasp on the subject, talk to your doctor. If you feel you know much more about this than your doctor, or he or she doesn't appreciate that you've been researching or respect your knowledge, then ask for a referral to a specialist.

People understand that medical knowledge is so encompassing today that no one can be an expert on everything, but they do expect their doctor to be willing to learn all he can about their condition. Most people will choose a caring doctor who might not be an expert on their condition, but listens, over an expert doctor who's arrogant.

If your doctor does not agree with your opinion of your situation, nicely ask him to refer you to a book or medical article that explains his point of view. If he can't do it then ask for a referral.

Two books we recommend are *Screaming to Be Heard* and *It's My Ovaries, Stupid!* by Elizabeth Lee Vliet, M.D. If you read either one of these books you will be quite knowledgeable on the subject.

Melatonin: The Body Clock Hormone

Melatonin is a hormone, which is actually derived from serotonin and released by the pineal gland. It is mostly used as a sleep aid. It does increase the speed of falling asleep and the duration of sleep. Regularly taking melatonin for sleep can mess up the body's natural production of melatonin and actually worsen sleep in the long run. Melatonin also enhances weight gain, especially in females.

If you need a sleep aid it would be safer to take a straight sleeping medication such as Ambien or Sonata rather than a hormone. The only recommended use of melatonin is in the treatment of jet lag, to help reset the circadian rhythm. Most people purchase melatonin at health stores without their doctor's knowledge. Please talk to your doctor before beginning or continuing melatonin.

Hormones, like genes, are another example of God's infinite wisdom and the intricate detail He created in us. Even though this chapter focused on what can happen when they don't work right, amazingly over 99.99 percent of the time as a whole they work perfectly. If they didn't, you wouldn't be here.

We conclude this chapter with an interesting, true case study that illustrates the principles of this chapter.

John and Susan's Story

Susan's husband John had spent weeks planning her fiftieth birthday surprise party, and the day was finally here. They would drive to an elegant lodge nestled on a lake for a weekend getaway. At least that's what Susan thought; the surprise was ten couples would also meet them there. There would be dinner, dancing, and lots of visiting for the mutual friends.

Susan looked forward to the getaway, not because of the dancing and so forth, but for the relaxation aspect. She had felt extremely tired the last six months and had even joked that "her get up and go had got up and went."

Her family physician checked her for mononucleosis, but all the tests were negative. He said it could be menopause as well because her menstrual periods had become very irregular. Susan had been dieting as well, but was unable to lose weight. This really bothered her when she tried on her dress for the birthday dinner and it didn't fit anymore. She wanted to cry and just stay home.

On the two-hour drive to the lodge she kept telling John to turn up the heat in the car. He finally said, "I can't take it any hotter, honey. You must have ice in your veins." He remarked on how she kept the heat on at home, even on warm days.

"My mother was like that," Susan snapped back. "Her doctor said our family is cold blooded."

"Let's don't fight," John said. "I want you to have a fun weekend. You just don't seem to enjoy life anymore."

"I don't know what's wrong with me," said Susan. "I feel like I'm turning into my mother. I'm turning 50, but I'm gaining weight, losing energy, my hair is starting to fall out, my skin is dry and flaking off like crazy, my face looks like it's holding water, and I've even started using laxatives to go to the bathroom. Something is wrong with me. My doctor says it could be menopause, but my other friends didn't go through all this. What's worse is I have no energy and sometimes wish I could go to bed and not wake up."

During the weekend Susan shared her health concerns with some of the other women there. A long-time friend insisted Susan see her physician when she got home. She did the next week and he ran a barrage of blood tests and did a thorough physical exam. Two days later he called and told Susan her thyroid hormone was low. Hypothyroidism explained most of her new symptoms.

He started her on replacement thyroid hormone and almost immediately she felt more energized. Over the next several weeks her weight decreased, skin softened back up, and hair stopped falling out. Susan felt like a 50-year-old now, rather than her mother. (In retrospect Susan wondered if her mother had suffered from low thyroid, but never had it diagnosed.)

John was glad to have "his" Susan back, and also glad that she wasn't running him out of the house with the heat set on 85 degrees anymore.

Chapter Ten

Nutrients, Vitamins and Blue Genes

I have had a few clients with dangerous hobbies and behaviors that range from refusing to wear a seat belt to driving a motorcycle reck-lessly—weaving between cars at top speed without a helmet. As a psy-chiatrist, I try to determine if these clients have a death wish, or just feel so entitled that they think they are immune to death. Some may actually be so extremely afraid of death—the ultimate loss of control—that they do dangerous things as an overreaction to their fears. They are trying to prove to themselves that they can defy death.

Believe it or not, when I ask why they risk dying in these ways, many give me a theological excuse, saying, "There is a day that God picked for me to die, and nothing I do will make it come sooner or later than that day."

"God definitely knows what day you are going to die," I reply, "but what if you get to heaven and find out He gave you an enormous influence over that day too, and He let you die 40 years early because you refused to wear a helmet when you raced down the highway on your motorcycle? The Bible says (in the first chapter of James) that God

never tempts anyone to sin. The Bible also describes people who committed suicide. If whoever taught you your theology is right, then if these people had not committed suicide, God would have had to make a tree fall on their heads or something else to make sure they died on the correct day."

It is definitely human nature to not want to accept responsibility.

Even though I am a busy doctor, taking care of everyone else in a thorough manner, I have often been irresponsible when it comes to taking care of my own health. It sure would be wonderful to me if I could never exercise, eat whatever I want, whenever I want, never have to take any medicines or vitamins, never see any other doctors (except socially), and still have perfect health.

Because of pretty good genes, I almost got away with it! When I turned 58, two of my best friends, Dwight Johnson and Dave Mandt, encouraged me to get the first complete physical exam of my life (other than insurance physicals).

I had never even had a regular family doctor and in 30 years had missed only three days of work due to illness. Plus, I am a physician and should know if anything is wrong. At least, I naively thought so.

But my friends insisted, so out of peer pressure I made an appointment. The internal medicine specialist I selected said my physical exam was fine, but she was disturbed by some of my lab results from the blood they had drawn and tested. She sent me to both a gastroenterologist and a cardiologist.

The gastroenterologist found a pre-cancerous growth, which he removed. So that alone may very well have added 30 years to my life.

(Most people I know hate to get those colon exams, and many men dislike getting the prostate checked. But these exams are not that bad, and they may save your life too. And since most male cancers are in *that general vicinity, and most are curable, let's do the loving thing for ourselves and our families, and, yes, even for continuing service to God, and catch these diseases early, when they are easier to treat.)*

The cardiologist found a high cardiac C-reactive protein (CRP) and a clearly elevated homocysteine level, which meant I probably had an increased risk for a heart attack or stroke. My cholesterol was also high. He told me that I was probably eating too many unhealthy carbohydrates, which would cause my body to put out too much insulin. The insulin was probably causing inflammation in my blood vessels, shown by the high CRP.

The cardiologist said if it went untreated, I could die sooner from a heart attack or a stroke.

"How much sooner?" I asked, so I could make an educated vote on whether it was worth giving up on one of my primary pleasures in life—carbs!

"I don't know," he said with a laugh, seeing where my irresponsible brain was leading me. "Could even be in the next five years!"

That got my attention. I was scared. I believe I will go to heaven when I die, but I still sort of like doing the things I am used to here on earth for some reason. He gave me a prescription for a statin (a cholesterol-lowering medicine that could help reduce the inflammation) but encouraged me to hold off on taking it for two or three months while trying a combination of exercise, diet, and vitamins and supplements, including folic acid, fish oil, B6, B12, and some others that he thought might help bring the homocysteine and CRP back down to normal.

He said we would retest my labs in about 10 weeks, and if they were not normal yet, I should take the cholesterol-lowering medicine. He also told me that since I was apparently so carbohydrate sensitive, I should eat fewer than 100 grams of carbohydrate per day (many foods today have the number of carbs listed on the label). He told me more of the carbs should be in the form of fruits and vegetables, and fewer should be white carbs (white bread, donuts, pasta, potatoes, etc.).

When he told me basically to give up those white carbs, I almost felt like my best friend died! I literally grieved the loss. Then I really balked when he told me to get liquid vitamins whenever possible, because he felt they would have better absorption. (The Physicians Desk Reference Web site, 2005, *says that people over 60, in particular, often have trouble digesting tablets.)[1]*

"I don't want to take liquid vitamins if I don't have to," I griped. "I remember my mom giving me some liver oil or something when I was a kid, and it tasted so bad that I still dread it."

He said I could either have a daily teaspoonful of a liquid fish oil, for example, or multiple tablets or capsules of the same brand of fish oil. I gave in and bought liquids, and I was right—they tasted horrible, as I had feared.

Now I was really grieving. First I had to cut way down on foods that I hope we will have for eternity in heaven (Krispy Kreme Donuts, warm sourdough bread loaded with melting butter, honey, Mexican chips with salsa, buttered popcorn, rice, really loaded baked potatoes, etc.). Then I had to replace these heavenly foods with liquid vitamins that tasted like someone made them from some dead and decaying fish.

I was encouraged that my "extreme" sacrifices would be worth it all when I came upon a research study published in the Journal of Nutrition. *It showed that Swedish women, ages 45 to 70, who regularly took a normal vitamin pill of any kind, had a 33 percent reduced risk of having a first heart attack, and men in that same age range had a 22 percent lower risk.[2]*

Of course, part of this result could be because people who take vitamins are more responsible to do other healthy things in their lives. But I reasoned that the vitamins themselves, logically, were probably at least part of the benefit.

The researchers themselves considered these possibilities, and factored in such elements as smoking, exercise, and diet, and came to the conclusion that the overall cardiac benefit of the vitamins alone was about a 20 percent reduction. But this was just one large study, so only time will tell if these results get duplicated over and over again.

Other researchers found the most helpful vitamins for cardiac health seemed to be folic acid, B6, B12, Vitamin C, and several others, which were in my cardiologist's list as well. I began to have a little hope.

I figured that if the vitamins themselves turned out somehow to be totally worthless, and all they did was remind me daily to take care of myself in other ways, it would still be worth taking them. And since God created vitamins within foods, apparently for our benefit from all the data I have gathered, then what are the odds that He created something worthless? Duh! Not too great! Of course, most poisons are also natural, so natural is not the same thing as being good for you. Sometimes natural will kill you.

The vitamins my cardiologist recommended were very expensive, since I bought so many of them individually. Dwight Johnson, my close friend who talked me into getting a physical in the first place, and his business partner, Robbie Gowdey, former personal assistant to Bill Bright of Campus Crusade for Christ, came through again. After many years of resisting their requests to work with them on vitamin development, I was finally convinced to help them develop a combination product to take all at once.

First they purchased a liquid vitamin formula from a large team of scientists. Then they allowed me, as a psychiatrist concerned about people's mental health, to add the essential nutrients needed for our brains to make the chemicals that maintain sanity, love, joy, and peace. I made sure everything on my cardiologist's list was in the new formula, including omega-3 fatty acids to replace the foul-tasting fish oil.

And a new nutritional supplement with about 200 ingredients was born. It was their baby, but I got to be the delivery doctor. After taking it for two months, along with eating fewer white carbs and doing more exercise, all my labs, including my homocysteine, came back to normal. (More information about this product can be found at http://www.meierclinics.org.)

As discussed in chapter two, brain amines are what God makes every day in our brains, if we eat enough of the building blocks to build them with. They are the most important chemicals in our entire bodies. They give us sanity, love, joy, peace, patience, and even help direct our thoughts and emotions.

Most people maintain adequate levels of the brain chemicals responsible for sanity, as well as experiencing love, joy, and peace through the spiritual disciplines, forgiveness, confessing our faults to one another, and grieving our losses. And even if we deplete our own brain chemicals by holding grudges or excessive shame, the spiritual things listed above will usually restore those chemicals.

The exception to this general rule would be individuals who are genetically prone to low serotonin levels or other problems with brain chemistry that might predispose them to depression, bipolar disorder, delusions, and other disorders. While diligent prayer, Bible study and wise counsel will draw them close to God and help them live wisely, it may not restore their brain chemistry to normal—just as many godly people need thyroid supplementation, insulin, or other medications to survive. Before scientists discovered how to replace thyroid hormone or insulin, for example, people who were deficient in these hormones (whether because of heredity or for other reasons) became ill and eventually died.

We are extremely fortunate to be living in an era in which there are newer and safer psychiatric medications developed every few months, allowing us to treat so many problems successfully, including

suicidal depressions, panic attacks, delusions, hallucinations, obsessive-
compulsive disorder, ADHD, and mood swings. I love being a psychia-
trist in this era.

—PAUL MEIER, M.D.

THE STATE OF NUTRITION TODAY

I (Dr. Meier) have often heard the statement that adults and teens in America today are the most overfed and undernourished people our nation has ever experienced. Could this really be true? I recently asked Dr. Walt Larimore for help in answering this question. I asked him why he thought today's younger generation was overfed and undernourished.

Walt sent me the following response, taken from his most recent nutritional book, *Supersized Kids:*

- On average, teens eat almost 300 calories more per day and burn about 300 calories less a day than we did twenty years ago. And where do those 600 extra calories go? Our body stores them as fat. When you consider that an additional 100 calories a day can mean an extra ten pounds a year, it's not hard to see how our kids can so easily gain an unhealthy thirty pounds or more!
- The serving size of an average soft drink increased from 13 ounces (144 calories) in 1977 to almost 20 ounces (with 15 tea-spoons of sugar and 250 calories) in 1998.
- Cheeseburgers grew from 5.8 ounces (397 calories) in 1977 to 7.3 ounces (533 calories) in 1998.
- Some researchers contend that eating fast foods can become addictive. "New and potentially explosive findings on the biologi-cal effects of fast food suggest that eating yourself into obesity isn't simply down to a lack of self-control," said one scientist. As body fat increases, people appear to become increasingly

insensitive to hormones that help to control their eating. The more fast food you eat, the less you may feel like you're eating.

- Most soft drinks contain something called "high fructose corn syrup," a cheap sweetener discovered in the early 1970s. Over the past fifteen years, the nation's consumption of this substance has grown by 250 percent; some experts estimate that we get as much as nine percent of our daily calories from fructose. But researchers at the University of Michigan have concluded that fructose in high levels elevates dangerous triglycerides by as much as 32 percent and slows down the body's fat burning and storage system. Result? Weight gain.

- Children who watch TV tend to burn fewer calories per minute than children involved in almost any other activity—not only fewer than those engaged in active play, but also fewer than those who read or "do nothing." In fact, the child watching TV burns almost as few calories as a sleeping child—and the heavier the child, the more grave the effect. For children of normal weight, TV watching triggers a twelve percent drop in metabolism. Obese children have a sixteen percent drop in metabolism.[3]

WHAT YOUR BODY AND BRAIN NATURALLY NEED

The Bible calls our bodies the "temples of the Holy Spirit." God designed our bodies so that if we took reasonable care of our "temples" by getting enough sleep, eating the right foods, and obeying all the "one another" concepts in Scripture (confessing our faults one to another, speaking the truth in love to each other, loving one another, etc.), then our serotonin levels will stay high and our spirits will as well.

But it is very important to realize that some people do all of the above and still suffer from suicidal depression because of their *blue genes*. For them, antidepressants *and* adequate nutritional intake of the essential amino acids, especially tryptophan and phenylalanine, and adequate vitamin B6 intake are a must, in order for the spiritual disciplines to do what they normally do in our brains.

Many people eating the typical modern Western diet don't eat enough of the foods that are rich in tryptophan, to get plenty of the essential amino acids needed for our brains to be able to make the primary "power steering fluid," called serotonin. I (Dr. Meier) did some of the original research on tryptophan and serotonin for Michigan State University for my master's thesis in cardiovascular physiology, all the way back in 1968.

Some Christians think that whenever our brains' "power steering fluid"—serotonin—gets low, which nearly always occurs when we feel severely depressed, then we should be able to pray and think it back to normal. And do you know what? For some people that is actually true! Even many depressed people.

If there is a spiritual cause of the serotonin depletion, like buried anger or excessive shame, then resolving these things spiritually and for-giveness will eventually straighten out the serotonin level in most cases. Psychiatrists call depression "anger turned inward."

The trouble comes when Christians become simplistic and think this is always the case, and it isn't. Those who inherit a low serotonin level can-not pray it or think it up to normal. Proper nutrition, to build it up, and medication, to block the reuptake sites and force it to accumulate to a normal level, will bring joy and peace to a person who was biochemically suicidal a few weeks earlier.

So, as my radio listeners often hear me say, "If your car runs out of power steering fluid, go ahead and pray, but call Triple-A." And if your brain gets so low on its power steering fluid that you are having anxious and depressed thoughts, you need to deal with this in several ways: pray, get counseling, eat right (or take supplements with the essential amino acids), and take an antidepressant while you are doing the spiritual disci-plines as well. If you have adequate nutrition, but are mildly depressed due to spiritual causes, then you probably won't need medicine, just the spiritual growth.

In my personal observations of my eating disorder patients for the past 30 years, I have noticed that we humans often seem to do the same thing deer do. In Colorado, when the deep snows cover many of the healthy foods that deer like to eat, some deer become vitamin deficient and will eat the bark off of certain types of birch trees. (Talk about vitamins tasting bad!)

When we lack certain vitamins, I suspect that our bodies sense it, and we crave foods that we unconsciously sense contain those vitamins. We may even binge eat. Chocolates are high in tryptophan, so we may crave more chocolates when depressed and serotonin depleted, since serotonin is built from tryptophan. By eating excellent foods, we won't have any of these key vitamins missing, so we may eliminate at least one cause of binge eating.

As you investigate improved nutrition, be aware that lots of vitamins and nutritional products are not what they claim to be. For instance, Dr. Walt Larimore writes in his book, *Alternative Medicine:*

> The *Los Angeles Times* commissioned a study to examine St. John's wort, an herb known to be effective against some forms of mild to moderate general depression. *Times* reporters purchased the ten most common brands from several retail outlets, then had the pills tested by an independent laboratory. The results were startling. Only one had between 90 and 110 percent of what the label indicated (an acceptable standard for over-the-counter products, based on the German standards)....One manufacturer's pills had only 20 percent of the amount of active ingredient claimed on the label. Two others had a third more than the labels claimed. ("Remedy's U.S. Sales Zoom, But Quality Control Lags," by Terence Monmaney, *Los Angeles Times*, August 31, 1998, from website.)[4]

The four authors of this book feel that we cannot overemphasize the importance of proper nutrition and the role it plays in our physical and emotional health. Eating a balanced diet, with plenty of vitamins and minerals, would benefit everyone, not just those who fall into the category of having "blue genes."

Especially seek out foods or vitamins that contain three of the essential amino acids—tryptophan, phenylalanine, and tyrosine—as well as an essential nutrient, choline. Doing so will at the least assist you toward restoring your brain chemicals to normal levels, as if you were filling up your brain with its "power steering fluid."

WHERE TO FIND IT?

1. Tryptophan: dairy products, beef, turkey, bananas, poultry, barley, brown rice, fish, soybeans, and peanuts.

2. Phenylalanine: animal and vegetable proteins, vegetables, and juices. It is also found in fermented foods such as yogurt and miso.

3. Tyrosine: animal and vegetable proteins, vegetables, juices, and fermented foods such as yogurt and miso.

4. Choline: usually made from phenylalanine, but also widely distributed in many foods. Choline is important for normal membrane function and acetylcholine synthesis. The choline requirement for adults is 550 mg per day. Foods with the highest total choline concentration (mg/100 g) are: beef liver (418), chicken liver (290), eggs (251), wheat germ (152), bacon (125), dried soybeans (116), and pork (103). (This information is from the American Society for Nutritional Sciences *Journal of Nutrition,* 133:1302-1307, May 2003.)

5. Vitamin B6: meat, fish, poultry, dried beans, bananas, potatoes, raisins, and dried figs, dates, and prunes. (Information from the 2005 PDR Web site.)

For further reading on the subject of nutrition, we recommend the following five books:

1. *The Complete Guide to Family Health, Nutrition, and Fitness* (available April 2006 from Focus on the Family and Tyndale House Publishers)

2. *10 Essentials of Highly Healthy People,* by Walt Larimore, M.D. (Zondervan)

3. *Alternative Medicine,* by Walt Larimore, M.D. and Donal O'Mathuna, Ph.D. (Zondervan)

4. *Supersized Kids,* by Walt Larimore, M.D. and Cheryl Flynt, M.P.H., R.D. (Center Street Publishers)

5. *Examining Alternative Medicine,* by Paul Reisser, M.D. (Inter-Varsity Press)

All four authors of this book would like to conclude this chapter with strong encouragement and a strong warning to every reader. God uses doctors, such as Dr. Luke, who wrote the Book of Acts and accompanied the apostle Paul on his missionary journeys. God uses medicines, such as the Balm of Gilead, mentioned in the Old Testament, and medicinal wine for Timothy's stomach problems, mentioned in the New Testament. So we encourage all readers to love and respect yourself and respect your body, the temple of the Holy Spirit. Eat, sleep, relax, pray, meditate, and get regular physical exams by a competent physician.

Don't forget to laugh; wise King Solomon said that "a cheerful heart is good medicine" (Proverbs 17:22). This verse teaches us not only that medicine is often good for you, but also that laughter is also good for you, like a medicine.

God also blesses us with enough common sense to maintain our cars and find excellent mechanics when our cars break down. He also gives us the wisdom to pray for His healing for any and all physical and emotional illnesses.

If we have a serious problem, He encourages us to have the elders of our church come and anoint us with oil and pray for our healing. But God shows us that sometimes it is best for Him to heal us supernaturally, and sometimes it helps us be more humble if He doesn't. God even turned down the apostle Paul three times and told him to live with whatever disease he had.

If you were lost at sea in a rowboat, and you suddenly saw the shore, would you pray to God or row to shore? Some Christians say one; some say the other. But the correct biblical answer is to do both. As the apostle Paul says in Philippians 4:13, "I can do everything through him who gives me strength." This verse shows us we can't do it without God's strength, but it also shows us He doesn't want to spoil us by doing everything for us. He likes us to be a team. He would want us to row to shore and ask Him for the strength to make it.

Likewise, if you are ill, "pray to God but row to shore." If you have an illness, pray for healing and ask others to pray for you. See the best physician you can. If you need to see a counselor, then be sure to see a Bible-believing Christian to work on your soul.

If you are on medications for a disease of any kind, stay on them. Even if you don't think you need the medicines any longer, don't try to be your own doctor. Follow your doctor's advice. He or she can help you decide whether and when you can try going off that medicine.[5]

NOTES

1. *Physician's Desk Reference,* 2005 edition (from Web site: pdrhealth.com)

2. C. Holmquist, S. Larsson, A. Wolk, U. de Faire, *Journal of Nutrition* 133: 2650-2654, 2003 (published by the American Society for Nutritional Sciences: Bethesda, MD)

3. *Supersized Kids: How to Rescue Your Child from the Obesity Threat,* Walt Larimore, M.D. and Cheryl Flynt, M.P.H., R.D., (Center Street Publishers: Nashville, TN), 2005

4. *Alternative Medicine,* Walt Larimore, M.D. and Donal O'Mathuna, Ph.D., (Zondervan: Grand Rapids, MI), 2001

5. Further information and background sources used in this chapter can be found at http://www.meierclinics.org.

Chapter Eleven

Blue Genes and the Future of the World

They sailed to the region of the Gerasenes, which is across the lake from Galilee. When Jesus stepped ashore, he was met by a demon-possessed man from the town. For a long time this man had not worn clothes or lived in a house, but had lived in the tombs. When he saw Jesus, he cried out and fell at his feet, shouting at the top of his voice, "What do you want with me, Jesus, Son of the Most High God? I beg you, don't torture me!" For Jesus had commanded the evil spirit to come out of the man. Many times it had seized him, and though he was chained hand and foot and kept under guard, he had broken his chains and had been driven by the demon into solitary places.

Jesus asked him, "What is your name?"

"Legion," he replied, because many demons had gone into him. And they begged him repeatedly not to order them to go into the Abyss.

A large herd of pigs was feeding there on the hillside. The demons begged Jesus to let them go into them, and he gave them permission. When the demons came out of the man, they went into the pigs, and the herd rushed down the steep bank into the lake and was drowned.

When those tending the pigs saw what had happened, they ran off and reported this in the town and countryside, and the people went out to see what had happened. When they came to Jesus, they found the man from whom the demons had gone out, sitting at Jesus' feet, dressed and in his right mind; and they were afraid. Those who had seen it told the people how the demon-possessed man had been cured.

—Luke 8:26-36

Mental illness has always carried a stigma. For thousands of years and up to the present, many have linked mental illness to demon possession or oppression, even though only one demon-possessed person in the entire Bible resembled a mentally ill person. That was the demoniac whose story is told above. The rest had either special demonic gifts or physical illnesses, such as seizure disorders.

Even today, with our increased understanding and treatment of mental illness, many people say they feel safer with the mentally ill off the streets and out of sight. We still read newspaper stories about people who put up fierce resistance when they learn a halfway home for the mentally ill is planned for their neighborhood.

The History of Treating Blue Genes

Writings from as late as the nineteenth century detail the torture the mentally ill were put through, some of it in the name of science to find a cure. These patients were chained up, fed strange diets, and immersed in freezing water, along with many other cruel treatments. In the eighteenth century a large insane asylum outside London supported itself by charging the wealthy a fee to tour the place on Sunday afternoons. The patients were kept in cages with hay for a floor. Many of them acted like animals, which was the entertainment draw. Journals from visitors record that it was commonplace to see these patients engaged in sexual activity or eating their own feces.

Fifty years ago there were no psychiatric medications. Family members cared for the mentally ill at home. If that became too difficult, they were sent to live in state hospitals. On any specific day before 1955, there were five times as many people in mental hospitals as in medical hospitals. These state institutions were huge and overcrowded, and the sanitary conditions in most became deplorable. A few are still left, but most are empty.

I had the privilege of working at Eastern State Hospital (ESH) in Vinita, Oklahoma, during my residency. Vinita is a tiny town, but it has two claims to fame: It has the largest McDonald's in the world, and it's the hometown of Phil McGraw (Dr. Phil). ESH was built in 1918 to house the psychiatrically ill and get them out of the city of Tulsa. Oklahoma governor Frank Keating closed down most of the facility several years ago.

In its heyday, ESH was a thriving community. Many of the residents spent their entire lives there. The community had gardens, and the patients grew and cooked their own food, made their own clothes, and kept the grounds mowed and the buildings clean. They also had their own church and gymnasium. The campus was out in the country. There were no fences around the perimeter because the residents knew that if they ran away, there was nowhere to go but cow pastures. Road signs asked drivers not to pick up hitchhikers.

Then the government (with pressure from groups like the ACLU) passed a law that made it illegal for mentally ill people to work. Now the state had to hire "healthy" people to do the jobs associated with the facility, while the residents could only sit around and smoke cigarettes. The groups who thought they were helping the mentally ill actually harmed most of them. They took away their jobs, which had given many their pride, purpose, and sense of belonging to the community.

In 1955, a new, promising drug for curing tuberculosis (TB) was tested on state hospital residents. This was legitimate because the TB rate was high in these hospitals due to the overcrowding. The drug didn't work that well for TB, but many of the patients who took it became normal again. This wonder drug was Thorazine, and 1955 started the period known as "The Exodus." Millions of people previously destined to spend the rest of their lives in a mental institution were suddenly able to go home. The state hospitals were cleared out.

—Todd Clements, M.D.

The 1960s and 70s ushered in the first medical treatments for depression. Drugs known as monoamine oxidase inhibitors (MAOIs) and tricyclic acids (TCAs) were found to improve depression dramatically. These medications, however, had a huge number of side effects, and some people claimed that the meds made them feel worse than the depression did. These drugs were also fatal in overdose, which created a complex dilemma for doctors: Should they give someone who was already suicidal what amounted to a lethal dose of medication?

Lithium was the mainstay of bipolar treatment, along with electroconvulsive therapy (ECT), and both are still sometimes used today.

The late 1980s and early 90s witnessed a dramatic change in psychiatric medication. Novel drugs came to market that were non-lethal in overdose, carried fewer side effects, and worked on specific neurotransmitters in the brain. Prozac was the prototype; it worked solely on serotonin.

The 1990s also witnessed an improvement in bipolar medications. The role of GABA in moods and anxiety was further defined. Better antipsychotics were also created that not only improved paranoia and psychosis, but also depression, anxiety, and mania.

In addition to the question of treatment, the underlying question was "What actually causes these problems? What factors lead to an imbalance of serotonin, dopamine, norepinephrine, GABA, and other brain chemicals?" We've known for over a century that environment and life choices have a profound effect on mental health. There has long been speculation that genetics were also involved in personality as well as physical traits. We acknowledge this by statements such as, "You act just like your mother." Only in the last few decades have we started substantiating "blue genes."

FUTURE TREATMENTS

Now that we know about "blue genes," how will that knowledge affect future treatments? The current project to map the human genome will change medicine and ethics forever. This huge task, which thousands of scientists from numerous countries are coming together to complete, is an attempt to unlock our genetic map. Specifically, they want to determine where every gene is located on our chromosomes.

Doctors have the ability to remove a baby's cells which float in amniotic fluid and know every one of the child's genes before birth. We can already test for Downs syndrome in this way. Soon this method, called amniocentesis, will be much more advanced and give us the ability to predict numerous future diseases. A doctor may be able to tell if an unborn baby will have problems with depression, bipolar disorder, or perhaps schizophrenia. He will also be able to tell if a child has the genes for Alzheimer's disease or breast cancer.

THE EDGE OF THE ABYSS

So what happens when the doctor says, "I'm sorry, but your daughter will be severely mentally retarded"? Or what if you are told your unborn son will have muscular dystrophy, causing him to be wheelchair bound before age 10 and most likely dead before his teens? Could this knowledge, meant to improve and save lives, result in more abortions? No doubt.

Some genetic defects will be curable, or at least we'll be able to "neutralize" them. This is where the hope in stem-cell research lies, the kind that President Bush approved, not the creation of new life in the form of embryos which would exist only to be destroyed later.

While the U.S. government proceeds cautiously, knowing that embryonic cell research will encourage more abortions, many foreign countries, and many politicians within our own country, don't really care if young lives are aborted.

> *At the risk of sounding alarmist, shades of Adolph Hitler! He got abortions approved in Nazi Germany, devaluing human life. Then he approved of killing "defective" infants, a further devaluation.*
>
> *I wrote the previous sentence late one night, thankful that our world was probably still a long way off from actually allowing doctors to murder infants with blue genes (genetic defects). Then, when my alarm clock radio woke me the next morning, National Public Radio was announcing that physicians in the Netherlands are now killing infants with spina bifida, with parental consent. They interviewed a physician who explained why killing these babies is the "humane" thing to do. I was first stunned and then grief-stricken.*
>
> *How much of a step will it take for doctors to then kill adults with spina bifida or other genetic defects? Again, Hitler did that! Hitler told the German doctors to kill the mentally handicapped to purify the Aryan race's genetic pool. Then he eventually approved of killing Polish people and Jews, saying they were of inferior genetic makeup.*
>
> *All four authors of this book are against embryonic stem-cell research but totally understand how some well-intentioned people are in favor of embryonic stem-cell research to try to save lives, heal paraplegics, and so on. But there are other ways to do that same research without creating new embryos, which are young human lives, and then using and destroying them.*
>
> *Good people who favor this don't really realize that they would be leading society down the same slippery slope Hitler led Germany down in the 1930s and 40s. But we are sure that governments, along with*

private corporations, will march forward in full force with embryonic
stem cell development, research, and then destruction. It sounds so
appealing, destroying embryos to save the lives of adults, and it's a lot
more subtle than something like partial birth abortion, where a baby
is killed just as it's being born. But we hold to the truth that every
human life at every stage of development is of infinite worth, even with
blue genes in the genetic pool.

—PAUL MEIER, M.D.

BENEFITS OF STEM-CELL AND OTHER RESEARCH

The upside to stem-cell research is twofold. First, stem cells can be gleaned from umbilical cord cells and placental cells and other sources that don't involve taking a life. Second, scientists will continue to learn how to identify future diseases early and treat many blue genes. If your child has the genes for schizophrenia, treatment can be started before a psychotic break happens. This will probably prevent him from ever becoming psychotic.

We will also have the ability to know who will develop dementia. We can then start treating early, before the first symptoms, adding on years of quality life. In fact, most psychiatric disorders can be treated before they manifest, including depression, bipolar disorders, and obsessive-compulsive disorder. This will certainly lessen their impact or prevent them altogether.

Amazing new treatments in psychiatry are just around the corner. The whole approach to brain disorders is changing. Currently, psychiatric disorders are diagnosed by directly observing the person's behavior or asking questions in a structured interview or questionnaire. There are no lab tests yet that can diagnose, for instance, bipolar disorder. (Quacks will charge you thousands of dollars to check your hair follicle or fingernail or a blood or urine sample to diagnose bipolar disorder and other such things, but those tests are totally worthless.) But SPECT (single photon emission computed tomography) scans are now allowing psychiatrists to objectively diagnose many psychiatric disorders for the first time.

Likewise, computed tomography (CT) scans and magnetic resonance imaging (MRI) allow us to observe the brain's anatomy. Positron emission tomography (PET) and SPECT scans show us how the brain is functioning. These scans detect what areas of the brain are using the most glucose, hence are the most active (the brain uses glucose for energy).

SPECT scans can also detect how the rate of blood flow differs across the brain. The scans of anyone who has abused alcohol, pot, cocaine, or heroin for 10 years or longer will show large holes in the brain where the cells have died from substance abuse. These cells will never be recovered even if the person abstains from that moment on. (But at least he won't be killing off the rest of his brain cells so quickly.) It has been estimated that one shot of whiskey on an empty stomach will kill 2,000 brain cells permanently.

We now know that certain psychiatric symptoms are due to overactivity or underactivity in specific areas of the brain. For instance, an overactive limbic system relates to symptoms of depression. Overactivity in the area known as the cingulate gyri results in obsessive thoughts (like songs or commercials that won't leave your head) and compulsive behaviors (like counting things all the time, rechecking things several times needlessly, excessive hand washing, hoarding newspapers or antiques, repeated hair twirling, etc.).

Underactivity in the left temporal lobe is associated with anger problems. The proper medication and/or counseling therapy can correct all these abnormalities, thus relieving the psychiatric symptoms. Ten straight weeks on a higher-than-average dose of any of the newer serotonin medications will eliminate obsessive-compulsive traits most of the time. Sometimes these traits, even after 30 or 40 years of constantly having them, will cease within an hour or two after taking even a low dose of one of the newer powerful dopamine medications (called atypical antipsychotics, even though they are used for many disorders that do not involve psychosis).

Research continues to improve the reliability of SPECT technology. Within the next 10 years, this will become the primary method of diagnosing psychiatric illness. Specific treatments will target abnormally functioning areas of the brain. Both diagnosis and treatments will be much more specific. For instance, SPECT scans can already diagnose six different types of ADHD.

Future treatments will be designed to work faster and with fewer side effects. One problem with psychiatric treatment today is that many disorders take weeks or months to successfully treat as the medications gradually restore the proper level(s) of brain chemicals.

Neuroscience research is already exploring more direct ways to restore brain chemical levels and so reduce the healing time to a few days. Transmagnetic stimulation (TMS), for example, is undergoing clinical trials in the United States and Europe at the time of this writing. TMS focuses a beam of magnetic electricity to the brain. Here's an example of how TMS works: Serotonin is predominantly made in a small area of the brain called the median raphe. Stimulation of the median raphe by electricity sparks the neurons to start firing, which releases more serotonin.

In 10 years, though, even advances like TMS will probably be considered archaic, much as we now view the psychiatric treatments of 50 years ago.

COMPUTER CHIPS IN TREATMENT

Computer chips will soon become an integral part of psychiatry, as well as all other branches of medicine. Chips embedded in or under the scalp (no, not with "666" implanted in the chip!) can transmit electric signals that speed up or slow down activity in areas of the brain. We already use this technology in treating Parkinson's disease. Parkinson's is caused by a low level of dopamine in an area of the brain known as the substantia nigra. The actor Michael J. Fox, who suffers from Parkinson's, had surgery several years ago in which an electrode was placed in his brain to stimulate the substantia nigra to release more dopamine.

A blind man in Sweden recently had a computer chip placed in the part of the brain that controls sight (the occipital lobe located in the back of the brain). Electrodes protrude out of the back of his head and can hook up to a special pair of glasses. When he wears these glasses, the man can see! He can even drive! Some of the treatments that scientists are developing with computer chip technology are truly mind-boggling.

DRAWING THE LINE

Human beings shouldn't become robots, however. And a key question will be, "Where do you draw the line with these treatments?" Society will face increasing ethical dilemmas. Some factions will push toward "perfection." Governments could press to eliminate babies with genetic imperfections before they are born. Many will see it as merciful to abort any fetus at risk for serious disease.

People who disagree with this, believing that all life is sacred regardless of society's current standards, will be portrayed as cruel barbarians. We will be deemed as a bunch of idiots, totally out of touch with real knowledge, who enjoy watching "inferior" people suffer.

Discrimination will take a whole new form. Rather than skin color, ethnicity, or education, discrimination will be based on genetics. The 1997 movie *Gattaca* portrayed this well. In this film's futuristic society, those with inferior genetics are relegated to menial labor jobs and low social status. A person's genetic code permeates every sliver of civilization. People applying for any kind of job, school, or other position must submit a DNA sample.

CLONING

What about cloning human beings? Is it a future reality or wishful scientific dreaming? It probably is a reality. Many medical scientists and researchers are beginning to acknowledge this scary conclusion. No one knows yet how far away man is from this capability. Most scientists dismiss the claims of certain groups who brag that they are only a few years away from cloning people. This whole sector of science is shrouded in secrecy and deception, so no one really knows the truth.

There have already been some claims of successful animal cloning (e.g., "Dolly" the sheep). Critics say these are not true clones because of certain scientific qualifications. The future cloning of people might be imprecise as well, but this is irrelevant. The cold fact is that someone will be able to produce people in a lab, without regard to mother or father. There are likely to be artificial wombs by that time as well. Human beings could potentially be created out of DNA and grown until birth in a lab. This may sound like pure science fiction, but right now there are thousands of people spending millions of dollars, working around the clock, to make this happen. Remember, flying machines were also pure science fiction in the late 1800s.

Who in the world would want to clone human beings, and why would they want to do it? *Who?* Governments and the private sector. *Why?* Governments might do it for military purposes. What if you could clone a million Arnold Schwarzeneggers or General Pattons? They could be governmental property and start military training at a young age. What if you were a small country and had the ability to clone one million men who would be martyrs for their country? In 20 years your country would be a force to be reckoned with. Citizens would probably like this too, because now they wouldn't have to fight in wars, getting injured or killed—the clones could do it.

What if our government could clone Bill Gates or Mark Cuban several times? Could we stay ahead of the world in technology? The possibilities are almost endless for how governments could use clones—especially rogue governments.

What about the private sector? What if you had an eight-year-old daughter who was killed in an automobile accident? This happens every day. What if I said, "I can give you this child again, or at least her identical twin"? Would that not be enticing? What if you could raise an identical twin of yourself?

What if you could buy and raise Michael Jordan's clone? (Get ready for a large grocery bill.) What about the clone of a movie star? How would you like to have a daughter who looked like Cindy Crawford? What about a son with the personality of Robin Williams? You'd never have to leave the house for entertainment.

What about raising Billy Graham's clone as a son? What a potential heart and mind you could shape for God's use! The possibilities here in the private sector are endless as well. We haven't even discussed what ways evil individuals could and would use cloning. An extremely narcissistic male, for example, could clone a female version of himself to marry in the future and train her from birth that he is always right! How scary is that?

So what would life be like with human clones? Confusing and chaotic! If a single woman clones a child, is she then the mother? Who would be the father? Society would return to owning people like the slavery days before the Civil War, again devaluing human life. What about the people who have multiple clones? How could you tell a large number of look- and act-alikes apart?

What about crime? We use DNA evidence to convict and exonerate suspects today. What happens when one of the million Arnold Schwarzenegger clones—all with identical DNA—commits a murder? Eyewitnesses are no help because all the suspects look alike. And if one of these clones dies, how do you tell who exactly it is? My guess that answers all these questions is scary—embedded computer chips.

Dr. Clements's grandmother has an identical twin sister. Growing up, they fooled people all the time by pretending to be each other. His grandmother's sister would trick his grandfather when they were dating, pretending to be his grandmother on the phone. They even took college classes for each other. What about a world full of multiple sets of twins, triplets, and quadruplets? Mass mayhem.

Jesus said in Matthew 24, concerning the end time, that no one knows that hour except the Father. Some theologians believe God has not set an exact date for the second coming but rather has decided that when mankind reaches a certain level of depravity, it will be time to usher in the Tribulation. This would be in line with God's actions at the Tower of Babel and the Great Flood. Could human cloning (or rather, what people would do with human clones) be that point of depravity?

MADE IN GOD'S IMAGE

Back to the here and now. God has made mankind in His own image. This image is extremely complex and fascinating. Each person has around 25,000 genes that determine his or her physical body. Either God or the world controls the spirit. Man has been given control of his soul while here on earth. He can turn this control over to Jesus or continue to be his own master.

As we learn more about the genetic makeup of human beings, there is huge potential for good in the fact that we will be able to identify and correct major ailments that have plagued people for centuries. But this knowledge also brings in the potential for horrendous evil. The knowledge itself is neutral—it's what we do with it that matters. Who would have dreamed of the knowledge of the Internet only a generation ago? This same knowledge that is used for downloading a sermon or prayer, or for playing a beautiful hymn, is also used for viewing pornography and promoting prostitution.

People often ask, "Why would a God who is total love allow people, made in His image, to inherit blue genes that cause suffering?" We don't know. But we are excited about our ability in the near future to better treat such genetic problems and also concerned about the various ways in which that ability might be misused. And we know that one day God will answer this question and so many others.

Chapter Twelve

Dos and Don'ts: Helping Families with Blue Genes

Tom Patterson was a good, godly, creative, loving family man. He was active in a healthy local church. He spent a reasonable amount of time with his wife and children. Ambitious and willing to take risks, he started his own computer software business and within a few years was making two million dollars a year.

But his family did not live extravagantly. He gave large amounts of money to his church and to various mission groups. He stayed godly and humble and didn't let success ruin him like it does so many people.

But Tom had an inherited a "blue gene" illness: Bipolar I, with psychosis, that had never shown up at all in his life until age 36. No one would have ever suspected that a humble, godly, loving man like Tom could lose touch with reality within a couple of days. Tom had several bipolar relatives, but assumed he had not inherited it.

At age 36, Tom became manic, with arrogance, over-confidence, grandiosity, extreme joy, and creative ideas that seemed brilliant to him but were actually not brilliant at all. He also had racing thoughts, rapid speech, and irritability at anyone who disagreed with him, insomnia, and hyper motor activity (unable to sit still and racing from one project to the next).

Godly people, when manic, do ungodly things and have no control over them. Their brain chemicals are imbalanced and they do not know what they are doing. Therefore, they have almost no control over their behavior. When Tom Patterson flipped totally out, he went to a large topless restaurant, bar and strip club in Houston and bought it from the owner on the spot, paying an exorbitant amount of money. Tom went on to have sexual activities with several of the dancers that night.

Tom had never done anything like this before. He was just manic. His family could not believe it; they were too stunned to know what to do for a few days. Then, as suddenly as Tom had become psychotic and happy, he turned psychotic and suicidal, reaching a painful depth of depression that was almost unbearable.

He had paranoid delusions that many strangers at the mall were talking about him. He even believed that people he saw on television were talking secretly about him or giving him dirty looks over the TV screen. He heard "demon voices" telling him to kill his family and himself, and he almost did it.

He had his pistol out and was loading it when his wife realized she had to do something dramatic to save herself and the children, as well as Tom. She called the police, which made Tom very angry. He pointed the gun at her and almost pulled the trigger, but she prayed and spoke softly and lovingly and calmed him down.

When the police came, he started to point the gun at them and they pulled theirs and were ready to shoot, as they must do in situations like this to protect themselves and others. I have had hundreds of suicidal patients in the past thirty years who said they would pull a gun on a police officer and fire to get the police officer to kill them. That way, *the death would not be classified as a suicide and their families would collect insurance.*

The police officers talked Tom down also, and got the gun away, handcuffed him, took him involuntarily to the state hospital, and medicated him against his will for a week or so, which brought him back to close to normal. Tom voluntarily came to our Day Program to figure out his bipolar problem and learn to deal with it and protect his family from its effects.

We persuaded him to change his checking account so only his wife could sign the checks. He had access to a limited amount of cash she allotted him each month by mutual agreement. Tom had to file for bankruptcy and sell his house and his business to pay for his purchase of the strip club. Since he was such a committed Christian, he refused to sell it to someone else to use in that manner, so he sold it for a very low price to someone who promised to use it for normal business.

Tom had also given huge tips to everyone, from the strippers to the McDonald's waitress, to whom he gave a fifty-dollar tip for a hamburger. He was really grandiose when manic and the worst person on the planet when depressed.

After a week at the state hospital, and three weeks at the Meier Day Program, where Dr. Clements or I saw him daily and adjusted his medications, Tom was doing better than he had ever done before— even before the illness appeared. He was bankrupt and embarrassed, but relieved when we told him it was not because of any sin in his life, just a chemical imbalance.

The healthy Tom was always optimistic and used the whole horrible experience to learn more about mental illness and how he could help others who were mentally ill. He returned to loving his wife and kids, became active in church, started up another successful computer business, and began living an even better life than he had before his blue genes disrupted his life.

But then, during a sermon at his church, Tom became quite

emotional and went forward at the alter call to ask for healing for his bipolar. The pastor prayed over him and declared to a thousand people in the pews that Tom had been healed of bipolar.

Now please do not get me wrong. I am a committed Christian psychiatrist. I believe Jesus can and sometimes does heal people of various things. I think, however, that people who demand that Jesus heal their particular disease are sinful, prideful, and entitled.

Within a few months off meds, Tom Patterson went manic for four days, and since only his wife could sign checks, he forged her name on a check and borrowed a large amount of money at a gambling casino in Louisiana and managed to bankrupt his family again financially, and again slept with the loose women there, giving them thousands of dollars in tips.

Then came the typical crash, suicidal pain, "demon voices," plans to kill his wife and kids and himself developing again, and so on. But this time his wife handled the situation quickly and got him arrested and locked up in a bed in a state hospital with restrainers on all four limbs to keep him from running away or getting in fights with the staff. The staff, trained in the Mandt system, never used restraints except briefly when they absolutely had to, to keep Tom from harming himself or the staff or the other patients.

Tom came to our Day Program again, so we could teach him a little practical theology about accepting the realities of life and death and disease.

His medications were easy. Todd Clements and I simply put him back on what had given him a great life for the three years prior to getting "healed." Within ten days, he was back to normal, and had to walk his family through all the pain again of filing bankruptcy, selling their home, selling his business, paying off the gambling debts before the mafia literally did come and break his legs or kill him, and start out working for someone else again.

Three years later, Tom was running a completely different business, earning two million dollars a year again, and serving God and his family faithfully.

Believe it or not, most of my bipolar patients do the same thing Tom did. They do well for a year or two, decide they hate taking meds for one reason or another, have a relapse, and then get back on the meds. Most of them have to go through this once or twice before they finally give in to the fact that they need lifelong medication.

—PAUL MEIER, M.D.

In dozens of years of treating thousands of people for bipolar illness, we do not know of a single case that God chose to heal. But a large number of them are having a huge impact on the world for Christ while taking medications to balance their brain chemicals.

We have known hundreds of people who grew up with Downs Syndrome, another "blue gene" of sorts. We don't know of a single case today that God chose to heal. Why not? In Jesus' day, He did heal impossible cases to show that He was really God. He even raised the dead. He restored withered hands. We have yet to see any evangelist restore someone's withered hand.

Everyone Jesus healed died of something else later. God is not weak. We just live in a fallen world, with dying bodies, failing organs and altered chemical imbalances. The Apostle Paul had an illness God refused to heal three times, so he accepted the disease as God's will, to keep him more humble.

Paul sent a letter to Timothy encouraging him to drink some wine as a medicine for an intestinal ailment. Paul could have "faith healed" Timothy, since God had given Paul the special ability to do that in this era of history for a particular reason, but Paul told Timothy to heal it himself in a slower way, by using medicinal wine, probably to kill off the bacteria causing the disturbance.

I saw a young lady just this week, Teresa, who loved her mother very much, but her mother was a member of a religious group who believed God promises to heal every disease if we have enough faith. They believe the harsh misperception that if the person dies from that disease, it is because of a lack of faith in the person with the disease and/or the people praying for healing. What a heap of false guilt laid on many innocent people who happen to be naïve enough to believe it.

Teresa's mom simply got poison ivy from pulling weeds in her back yard, not noticing the poison ivy woven in the weeds. Her body became swollen with a severe allergic reaction that could have been cured with a number of different medications, possibly even with over-the-counter Benadryl or even Tylenol-PM. But her mother refused meds and demanded that God heal her. She refused to listen to her daughter and others who loved her, and listened instead to the founder of her religious sect. And, of course, her mother died.

My client had pleaded with her mother to take the meds this one time, but her mother demanded that God do things her way, instead of using the common sense God had given her to get it fixed.

—PAUL MEIER, M.D.

What if Teresa's mother's car had broken down prior to her death, and quit working because the power steering fluid had a leak? Imagine her car stopping in the middle of the highway without being able to turn the car one way or the other. If the mother's religious beliefs were correct, she should stay in the car and pray for the power steering fluid leak to heal itself, and for the power steering fluid that leaked onto the highway to magically, by faith, fly back into the proper storage places.

There is no difference with mental health issues. Why would a loving God be less interested in your car running out of power steering fluid, a potentially dangerous situation, and your brain running out of its power steering fluid, serotonin, an equally potentially dangerous situation?

With a blue gene illness, the "power steering fluids" of your brain (that give you mental and physical power and steer you to use that power of thought and action to accomplish good in the world) are simply leaking out too fast. You inherited reuptake sites that leak. It is as simple as that.

So you take a SSRI antidepressant like Lexapro (SSRI stands for "selective serotonin reuptake inhibitor"), and it simply plugs up the leaks, so the serotonin God is making in your brain from the tryptophan and B6 stays in your brain. It is as simple as plugging off a leak in your power steering fluid location.

Within ten weeks the serotonin level gets high enough again for you to experience love, joy, peace, gentleness, meekness, and patience instead of bitterness, depression, anxiety, irritability, arrogance, and impatience. The latter are all the result of low serotonin levels caused either by genetics or by stress or by sin.

WHAT PEOPLE DO NOT NEED

For those of you reading this book who have never experienced a serious depression, it may be very difficult for you to imagine how horribly painful depression can be. But try to remember the last time you had the flu, with vomiting, muscle aches, sadness, tiredness, head-aches, etc.

When people are clinically depressed, they feel flu-like symptoms for months or even years and often for an entire lifetime. How disgusting it must be when these genetic victims, in great pain, hear their loved ones telling them to "snap out of it" or "pull yourself up by your bootstraps and be happy."

Pastor Frank Howard, for example, is a very successful Dallas pastor who came for help because he had been trying to overcome his lifelong depression. He has a great family, a great church that loves him dearly, and literally no logical reason to be depressed. So over the years, Pastor Howard had many church members give him simplistic advice or "biblical

Band-Aids" to give him a quick fix for his depression, which he admitted openly in his sermons and conversations.

A one-hour initial evaluation revealed that Pastor Howard had multiple relatives on both sides of his family who had depression, schizophrenia, alcoholism, and other problems. It appeared his depression was genetic, and within a few weeks on an SSRI, he did fine and "lived happily ever after"—except for the normal ups and downs and trials and tribulations of life in this world. He has been on antidepressants for seven years now, and the joy he experiences in life is spread to family members and those in his life and church.

The worst possible thing a depressed person could hear is, "Well, if you only trusted Jesus more, He would heal you of your depression and you wouldn't need any of those doctors or those medications." Is that what you would tell your mate or your child if that person was an insulin-dependant diabetic? Or if their car ran out of power steering fluid because of a leak? Would you lay a false guilt trip on them too?

Blue gene victims don't need biblical Band-Aids either. These include Bible verses often misinterpreted and taken out of context, such as Romans 8:28 quoted as, "All things work together for good to those who love God." This could imply the person is depressed because he or she doesn't love God enough. The person already feels like dying before experiencing the extra pain of false guilt for not loving God enough, when in reality it may be that he or she just inherited a low serotonin level only medications can correct.

WHAT PEOPLE DO NEED

People today need the same basics of life that people have always needed. They need God, and they need to love and be loved by a few fellow humans who know all their secrets and love them anyway. They need seven or eight hours of sleep a night to rebuild the serotonin in their brains. They need to eat plenty of the essential amino acids that become the brain chemicals that allow us to think and have feelings. They need exercise.

People need daily meditation on Scripture, even if only for a few minutes a day. Hebrews 10:24 says people also need to be regular attendees of a local church, where they get spiritually fed, take part in the sacraments (baptism and holy communion), and get lifelong emotional support. We physicians have observed that people who attend any church or synagogue or mosque once a week or more are significantly healthier physically and live about seven years longer than people who don't.

Because of modern research, we know that families that are intact, with both a mother and a father, and families who attend church weekly, and teens that attend a youth group regularly, have significantly better mental and physical health and life expectancy than those who grow up in a broken family system.

We also know from modern research that the foods we eat are processed more than ever before, and thus are less nutritious than fifty years ago. Without proper nutrition, we cannot think clearly and feel happy and at peace. Positive thinking and positive emotions require a sufficient supply, in our brains, of serotonin, norepinephrine, dopamine and GABA.

So people would benefit greatly by eating a more varied and healthier diet that includes larger quantities of bananas, green vegetables, turkey meat, dairy products, and so on. They would also benefit from vitamin and mineral supplements. (See chapter 10.)

Courage is another necessity for those seeking to overcome "blue genes" obstacles.

I had a client tell me just this morning that the only reason she did not kill herself was because she was "too chicken." But I corrected her immediately and honestly by reminding her, "No, it is the opposite. If you were more chicken, you would have committed suicide to end your

horrible pain. It was your great courage that enabled you to stay alive
even though your pain is so severe you feel like dying every day."

—PAUL MEIER, M.D.

———

When our staff teaches them the information in this book, they see that depression—even very severe bipolar depression—improves significantly even though it may require lifelong meds. They discover that the brain is just one more organ, like the pancreas or thyroid. If those glands are defective, the owners of those glands can still live close to normal lives on thyroid hormones or insulin. In the same way, people who inherit various "blue genes" can also live close to normal lives by using modern scientific discoveries to correct their chemical imbalances.

So if you need help, get it. If you are in a psychological prison, set yourself free. If your beloved family member or friend is in a blue gene prison, help set him free.

If you attend a church that is behind the times when it comes to modern science and medications and theology, try your best to educate them. If your church criticizes all use of any brain medications, then pray about whether or not God would prefer that you move to a different church to be with practical Christians who don't try to condemn or control you.

Proverbs chapter 9 tells us that if we rebuke a wise person, that person will love us for doing so. God also tells us in Proverbs 9 that if certain people are "foolish"—or paranoid in psychiatric terms—those foolish people will hate us for telling them the truth, so don't waste time with them.

And if you want to be truly wise, truly your own best friend, truly the most able person to love and be loved by your family and friends and yourself, and truly free from spiritual and emotional types of anxiety and depression, remember that you can't do it on your own. You need a higher power, and the only true higher power is Jesus.

We need the genius who created our serotonin, norepinephrine, dopamine and GABA. We need the genius who created our trillions of cells with thousand of components and enzymes in each and every cell, with each of our trillions of cells working smoothly like a complete factory with thirty thousand workers in every factory.

We are fearfully and wonderfully made, as David told us in Psalm 139. God said in Psalm 139 that He was thinking about YOU, specifically, last night when you fell asleep. He was thinking about you this morning, specifically, when you woke up. He will think about you lovingly so many times today that you can't even count them. So whom are you going to believe, your Heavenly Father or your earthly father or mother or cult leader or boss or mate?

God said in Psalm 139 that with one arm He is hugging you. He is trying to convince you this very moment that you are loved and lovable and that He longs to spend eternity with you. He wants you to know that He created you for His enjoyment, so He could spend eternity with you, bringing you everlasting joy and finally a feeling of loving and being loved, just the way you are.

God said in Psalm 139 that with His other arm He is using all sorts of secret ways to lead you in the right direction. How did this book get in your hands? We believe God led the authors to put it together and He led you to read it, apply it, and teach it to others, and separate yourself from abusers, even well-intentioned abusers.

Quit putting your self-concept in someone else's control. Decide right now to become your own best friend, never again saying anything negative to yourself that you would not say to your best friend if he or she made the same mistake. In fact, write today's date in the back of this book with a written pledge to yourself that you will become your own best friend from today forward. And start a personal relationship with Jesus, your creator, if you haven't already.

Trust Him to come into your life and use the blood He shed on the cross two thousand years ago to wash away all your true guilt and true shame. He died and rose again and lives in heaven, building you a personal "Heavenly Condo"—so He can enjoy you forever and so other believers in Him can enjoy you forever.

What about your sins? Jesus told the self-righteous legalists who wanted to kill a woman caught in adultery by throwing stones at her, "Whoever of you has never committed a sin, you should throw the first stone at her." Everybody there then dropped their stones, since they had all sinned. Then Jesus said lovingly to the adulteress, "If none of them condemn you, than I don't either, but go home and quit committing that sin."

Admit to God right now some of your specific sins. Don't worry, you can't surprise Him. He knows more about them than you do. You may know what sin you committed, but He knows what particular genetic factors and childhood factors made you more prone to commit that sin, and He even knows what group of unconscious motives influenced you.

A Note to Atheists

If you are an atheist and reading this book, know that we emphathize with you. It is possible your beliefs stem from "father issues." If your father was gone all the time or too busy for you, your brain may have tricked you into thinking there is no Heavenly Father either. To believe there is no creative God, while seeing His creation all around you, takes a lot more faith than it does to believe in a creative God. Or perhaps your father was such a jerk that you WISH he never existed, so you imagine God doesn't exist. But God does exist. A design implies a designer.

Think about it. Are you going to deny and repress your rage toward your earthly father and transfer that rage to God instead? Then you could continue to idealize your earthly father and become prejudiced against your Heavenly Father, deciding there isn't any God anyway. Or you can believe what God said about you and Him in Psalm 139.

Your parents and society may have taught you that you have to earn their love and acceptance. God says His love is unconditional. In Ephesians 2:8-9, God tells us the only way to get to Heaven is to have faith in what Jesus did, not it anything you ever did or didn't do.

Heaven is a gift. A relationship with your creator is a gift. Eternal life is a gift. Your forgiveness and your value as a human being is a gift. God says in that passage that if you tried to be good enough to get to Heaven, you would just add the sin of pride to your existing list, and brag about how good you are, like so many religious leaders do today.

Right this moment you are probably sitting on some sort of chair or couch. You are trusting it to hold you up. It may or it may not. It could break, right? But you are taking a chance on it. A reasonable chance. At the time of this publication, I will be a 60-year-old psychiatrist with a seminary degree who has been reading his Bible since he was 10, and I still have doubts sometimes because of my strict German father. So don't feel so bad if you do too.

John the Baptist was Jesus' cousin and grew up with Jesus and saw Jesus perform real miracles, like withered hands growing back. But when John the Baptist was preparing to be killed for Jesus, he had doubts too. He sent a letter to his cousin, Jesus, from prison asking Jesus to reassure him that Jesus really is the promised Messiah.

Jesus sent John word that He was raising the dead, healing the blind, and asked John, "Who do you think I am?" So John was satisfied and though he lost his life at Herod's hand, he gained eternity.

Talk to the Heavenly Father, and to His Son Jesus right now. Ask them to forgive you for your sins—all your sins, past, present and future. And if you are so mad at your dad that you are still an atheist and can't quite get yourself to do this yet, then please say this very safe prayer:

"God, if there is one, please make yourself known to me. I don't really think you are there. I think this life is all I will experience. If you do exist, I'm not sure if I would like you or hate you for all the pain you have allowed in my life. But if you do truly exist, then I do want to know you, even though I am afraid to do this because of past hurts.

Please help me. I ask you to make yourself known to me somehow. I will be waiting and watching for you, just in case you really do exist. Amen."

The Bible tells us that if anyone in the whole world seeks after righteousness, that person will certainly be filled with righteousness. So if you sincerely seek God, He will absolutely find you and bring you into a personal relationship with Him. May God—the Real One—truly bless you, and may God bless all those in the world who depend on Him as their Higher Power rather than themselves.

Now make a phone call or two and take care of your "blue genes," if you have any. Or give this message to someone you love.

FINAL ADVICE FOR FAMILIES WITH LOVED ONES DEALING WITH BLUE GENES

If you have a family member who is dealing with issues related to his or her "blue genes," you may find it useful to review this summary of principles from this book.

Don't enable your loved one. Speak the truth in love. If your loved one is paranoid and thinks the presidential news conference is all about him in secret code, you will not win the argument. You should do polite "reality orientation." Tell him that you personally do not believe the government would spend millions of dollars to send him secret messages when they could simply call on the phone. Then drop the subject. He won't believe you, but don't argue. If you pretend you believe him, you make his delusions more deeply entrenched. Don't ever do that.

If your loved one has OCD, dysthymia, recurrent major depressions, ADHD, bipolar illness, post-abortion syndrome, postpartum depression, chronic fatigue, or psychosis of any kind, insist on him or her getting quality professional help. Your loved one is a Mercedes, not an old, beat-up jalopy. You wouldn't take a new Mercedes that had a mechanical breakdown to a ninth-grade shop student to fix, would you? For best results, take him to a physician who is experienced and qualified to deal with the problems listed above.

Develop a good spiritual life with God and with your loved one. Loving and being loved, and having a clear conscience, will do more good than anything else spiritually to restore your soul and maximize the rebuilding of the necessary brain chemicals needed to function well.

Be aware of anger. Share it often but tactfully, and forgive by bedtime. Ephesians 4:26-27 tells us to go ahead and get angry without sinning but forgive by bedtime, so Satan will not have a foothold in our lives. In Old Testament commandments, Leviticus 19:17-19 tells people to get angry when a neighbor wrongs them, but share the angry feelings with that neighbor (as iron sharpens iron, so a friend sharpens the countenance of his friend), but never seek vengeance on a neighbor.

Encourage your blue-gene loved one to do everything for himself he possibly can. Making him dependent on you lowers his self-esteem and almost dooms him to failure. Galatians 6 tells us to carry each other's "overburdens" but to let everyone carry his own, normal emotional load (his knapsack).

Get help for yourself. Read books like this one, or *Love Is a Choice,* or *Unbreakable Bonds.* These are books that tell you how to have a full life regardless of circumstances. Become your own best friend.

Build a support group for you and your friend or relative with "blue genes." Make it similar to a Board of Directors that oversees a person's growth and mental health. Apply peer pressure to your loved one when he needs to quit, and welcome him home with open arms after he finishes rehab.

About the Authors

Paul Meier, M.D.

Author of over seventy books, Paul Meier is a pioneer in the integration of the genetic, psychological and spiritual nature of man, with advanced degrees in Human Physiology (Michigan State University), Medicine (The University of Arkansas Medical School), Psychiatry (Duke University Medical School), and biblical studies (begun at Trinity Evangelical Divinity School and completed at Dallas Theological Seminary). He taught full-time at Trinity Seminary in the Chicago area for eighteen months and at Dallas Theological Seminary for twelve years. He and his sister, Nancy Brown, founded the national chain of Meier Clinics, a non-profit, 501c3 organization (1-888-7-CLINIC; website: http://www.meier clinics.org.) He is also one of the developers of the To Your Health Liquid Vitamins and To Your Health Liquid Weight Management, available on the Meier Clinics website.

Dr. Meier has practiced psychiatry for over thirty years, has written over seventy books, and has trained missionaries, pastors and professional therapists in France, Germany, Greece, Israel, Cuba, Peru, Sweden, Norway and Denmark.

Dr. Meier co-authored one of the original books on the topic of code-pendency, *Love Is a Choice,* which sold over one million copies, co-authored *Happiness Is a Choice* in 1978 with Frank Minirth, M.D., and co-authored *Unbreakable Bonds: Practicing the Art of Loving and Being Loved,* with his daughter, Dr. Cheryl Meier (psychologist).

Visit Dr. Meier online at http://www.meierclinics.com.

Todd Clements, M.D.

Child, Adolescent and Adult Psychiatrist, former youth pastor, and president of all four of his medical classes, he was elected Chief Psychiatry resident by his peers at the University of Oklahoma Medical Center. He has served as co-host with Dr. Paul Meier of the Meier Clinic national radio program. Dr. Clements is a second cousin of Samuel L. Clemens, also known as literary legend Mark Twain.

Jean-Luc Bertrand, D.M.D.

With doctorates in medical dentistry and psychology, Dr. Bertrand is a writer, documentary producer, and former pro sports team owner in Paris, France, where he currently resides. He is founder of Generation Africa (www.generation-africa.net), which ministers to tens of thousands of AIDS orphans, and he is also Paul Meier's longtime prayer partner.

David Mandt, M.A.

Founder of the world-renowned Mandt System (Putting People First), which is one of the primary accrediting agencies for humane treatment of potentially violent patients, nursing home residents, orphans, etc., he has an M.A. in leadership development and is a former Green Beret with seminary training from Dallas Theological Seminary.